EXPLORING

ENGLISH

2

EXPLORING
ENGLISH
2

Tim Harris • Allan Rowe

Longman

Exploring English 2

A Pearson Education Company
Pearson Education
10 Bank Street
White Plains, NY 10606

Editorial director: Joanne Dresner
Acquisitions editor: Anne Boynton-Trigg
Production editor: Nik Winter
Text design: Curt Belshe
Cover design: Curt Belshe
Cover illustration: Allan Rowe

Library of Congress Cataloging-in-Publication Data

Harris, Tim.
    Exploring English/Tim Harris; illustrated by Allan Rowe.
        p.   cm.
    ISBN 0-201-82575-9 (bk. 1). —ISBN 0-201-82576-7 (bk. 2)
    1. English language—Textbooks for foreign speakers. I. Rowe,
Allan. II. Title   94-47408
PE1128.H347 1995   CIP
428.2'4—dc20

    18 19 20 – BAM – 06 05 04 03 02

To our families

Contents

Preface

Exploring English is a comprehensive, six-level course for adult and young adult students of English. It teaches all four language skills—listening, speaking, reading, and writing—with an emphasis on oral communication. The course combines a strong grammar base with in-depth coverage of language functions and life skills.

Exploring English:

Teaches grammar inductively. The basic structures are introduced in context through illustrated situations and dialogues. Students use the structures in talking about the situations and re-enacting the dialogues. They encounter each structure in a variety of contexts, including practice exercises, pair work activities, and readings. This repeated exposure enables students to make reliable and useful generalizations about the language. They develop a "language sense"—a feeling for words—that carries over into their daily use of English.

Includes language functions in every chapter from beginning through advanced levels. Guided conversations, discussions, and role plays provide varied opportunities to practice asking for and giving information, expressing likes and dislikes, agreeing and disagreeing, and so on.

Develops life skills in the areas most important to students: food, clothing, transportation, work, housing, and health care. Everyday life situations provide contexts for learning basic competencies: asking directions, taking a bus, buying food, shopping for clothes, and so on. Students progress from simpler tasks, such as describing occupations at the beginning level, to interviewing for jobs and discussing problems at work at more advanced levels.

Incorporates problem solving and critical thinking in many of the lessons, especially at the intermediate and advanced levels. The stories in *Exploring English* present a cast of colorful characters who get involved in all kinds of life problems, ranging from personal relationships to work-related issues to politics. Students develop critical-thinking skills as they discuss these problems, give their opinions, and try to find solutions. These discussions also provide many opportunities for students to talk about their own lives.

Provides extensive practice in listening comprehension through illustrated situations. Students are asked to describe each illustration in their own words before listening to the accompanying story (which appears on the reverse side of the page). Then they answer questions based on the story, while looking at the illustration. The students respond to what they see and hear without referring to a text, just as they would in actual conversation.

Offers students frequent opportunities for personal expression. The emphasis throughout *Exploring English* is on communication—encouraging students to use the language to express their own ideas and feelings. Free response questions in Books 1 and 2 give students the opportunity to talk about themselves using simple, straightforward English. Every chapter in Books 3–6 has a special section, called "One Step Further," that includes discussion topics such as work, leisure activities, cinema, travel, dating, and marriage. Ideas for role plays are also provided to give additional opportunities for free expression. The general themes are familiar to students because they draw on material already covered in the same chapter. Role plays give students a chance to interact spontaneously—perhaps the most important level of practice in developing communication skills.

Provides continuous review and reinforcement. Each chapter concludes with a review section and every fourth chapter is devoted entirely to review, allowing students to practice newly acquired language in different combinations.

Provides exposure to key structures that students will be learning at the next level. This material, included in a special unit called "Preview," can be introduced at any time during the course at the discretion of the teacher.

Presents attractive art that visually supports and is integral with the language being taught. Humorous and imaginative illustrations, in full color, make *Exploring English* fun for students. In addition, the richness of the art allows teachers to devise their own spin-off activities, increasing the teachability of each page.

Each volume of *Exploring English* is accompanied by a Workbook. The Workbook lessons are closely coordinated to the lessons in the Student Book. They provide additional writing practice using the same grammatical structures and vocabulary while expanding on basic functions and life skills. The activities range from sentence completion exercises to guided paragraph and composition writing.

Student Books and Workbooks include clear labels and directions for each activity. In addition, Teacher's Resource Manuals are available for each level. These Manuals provide step-by-step guidance for teaching each page, expansion activities, and answers to the exercises. Each student page is reproduced for easy reference.

Audiocassettes for each level featuring an entertaining variety of native voices round out the series. All of the dialogues, readings, and pronunciation exercises are included on the tapes.

Chapter 1

TOPICS
Daily routines
At the park
Meeting people

GRAMMAR
Simple present tense
Adverbs of frequency

FUNCTIONS
Describing daily habits and routines
Starting a conversation

WHAT'S HAPPENING HERE?

1

2

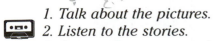

1. Talk about the pictures.
2. Listen to the stories.
3. Answer the story questions.

READING

1 Barbara Sherman is a secretary at the City Bank. She works every day from nine to five. She lives a long way from her job, and she doesn't drive a car. She always takes the bus to work.

1. Is Barbara a teacher or a secretary?
2. What hours does she work?
3. Does she live near her job?
4. Does she drive a car?
5. How does she go to work?

2 Sam Brown lives in Wickam City. Every morning he gets up at seven o'clock and takes a shower. Then he gets dressed and eats breakfast. Sam always has bananas and apple juice for breakfast.

1. Where does Sam live?
2. When does he get up?
3. Does he take a bath or a shower?
4. What does he do before breakfast?
5. What does he have for breakfast?

SIMPLE PRESENT TENSE: Affirmative

Barbara works at the bank.	They work every day.
She _____.	You _____.
Mr. Bascomb _____.	We _____.
He _____.	I _____.

PRACTICE • *Answer the questions.*

Does Barbara work from nine to five?
Yes, she works from nine to five every day.

Do the children walk to school?
Yes, they walk to school every day.

1. Does Peter drive to work?
2. Does Anne play the guitar?
3. Do Mr. and Mrs. Bascomb read the newspaper?
4. Does Sam eat bananas?
5. Does Mabel work in the garden?
6. Does Linda help her mother?
7. Do Barbara and Tino listen to the radio?
8. Does Tino drink coffee?
9. Does Barbara take the bus?

CONVERSATION

Listen and practice.

ANNE: Do you have a boyfriend, Barbara?

BARBARA: Yes, I do. His name's Tino.

ANNE: Tell me about him.

BARBARA: He's tall and handsome, and his family comes from Italy.

ANNE: Does he speak Italian?

BARBARA: Not with me. I don't understand a word of it.

ANNE: Does he have a good job?

BARBARA: Yes. He works for his father.

ANNE: What kind of business does his father have?

BARBARA: He has an Italian restaurant.

PRACTICE • *Read the first sentence. Then make a negative sentence for each picture.*

1. The Martinolis come from Italy.
   They don't come from France.

2. Mr. Martinoli speaks Italian.
   He doesn't speak French.

3. Anne and Barbara work at the bank.
   The don't work at the post office.

4. Barbara has blond hair.
   she has _____ brown hair.

5. Barney drives a taxi.
   He doesn't _____ a bus.

6. Mr. and Mrs. Golo like cats.
   The don't cat _____ dogs.

7. Jimmy and Linda live on Rock Street.
   The don't live _____ Pine Street.

8. Sam wears cowboy boots.
   He dog't has _____ tennis shoes.

Anne and Barbara live in Wickam City, and they work at the City Bank. After work they take the bus home. Mr. and Mrs. Farley also live in Wickam City and take the bus home from work. They work at the Regal Hotel.

PAIR WORK 1 • *Ask and answer questions about Anne and Barbara and the Farleys.*

A: **Do Anne and Barbara walk to work?**
B: **No, they don't. (They take the bus.)**

A: **Do they live a long way from the bank?**
B: **Yes, they do.**

A: **Does Anne wear glasses?**
B: **Yes, she does.**

A: **Does she have blond hair?**
B: **No, she doesn't. (She has brown hair.)**

1. Do Anne and Barbara live in Hollywood?
   Do they work at the City Bank?

2. Does Barbara have a car?
   Does she have a boyfriend?

3. Does Barbara have blond hair?
   Does she speak Italian?

4. Do Anne and Barbara like dogs?
   Do Mr. and Mrs. Farley like dogs?

5. Do the Farleys work at the bank?
   Do they take the bus to work?

6. Does Mr. Farley wear glasses?
   Does he wear a hat?

PAIR WORK 2 • *Ask and answer questions.*

live nearby?
A: **Do you live nearby?**
B: **Yes, I do.**   OR   **No, I don't. I live far from here.**

1. read the newspaper?
2. watch sports on TV?
3. like classical music?
4. play the piano?
5. speak Spanish?
6. have a big family?
7. live nearby?
8. walk to school?
9. take the bus?

Listen and repeat.

Otis <u>always</u> eats fruit and vegetables.

He <u>never</u> eats meat.

Johnny <u>often</u> goes to the movies.

He <u>seldom</u> watches television.

Mr. Bascomb <u>usually</u> drinks coffee.

He <u>sometimes</u> drinks tea.

ADVERBS OF FREQUENCY

They always get up at six o'clock.

____ usually _____.

____ often _____.

____ sometimes _____.

____ seldom _____.

____ never _____.

PRACTICE • Add *always, usually, often, sometimes, seldom*, or *never* to the sentences.

Otis eats meat. (never)
Otis never eats meat.

Mr. and Mrs. Bascomb listen to classical music. (always)
Mr. and Mrs. Bascomb always listen to classical music.

1. Mr. Bascomb drinks coffee. (usually)
2. He works on Sunday. (never)
3. He wears expensive clothes. (always)
4. I watch television. (often)
5. I go to the movies. (seldom)
6. I play basketball. (sometimes)
7. Marty gets up at seven o'clock. (usually)
8. He leaves the house in a hurry. (often)
9. He takes the bus to school. (always)
10. We eat at home. (seldom)
11. We go to Mom's Cafe. (often)
12. We have soup for lunch. (sometimes)

FREE RESPONSE • *Ask and answer questions using adverbs of frequency.*

A: Do you ever eat out?
B: **Yes, I often eat out.** OR **No, I seldom eat out. I usually eat at home.**

1. Do you ever get up at five o'clock?
2. Do you often take a hot shower?
3. Do you usually eat breakfast?
4. Do you ever drink coffee?
5. Do you always brush your teeth?
6. Do you sometimes listen to the radio?
7. Do you often read the newspaper?
8. Do you ever leave the house in a hurry?
9. Do you sometimes take the bus?
10. Do you usually study at the library?
11. Do you always do your homework?
12. Do you often help your friends?

Listen and practice.

MARTY: Good morning, Mrs. Golo.

MRS. GOLO: What time is it, Marty?

MARTY: It's half past nine.

MRS. GOLO: That's right. You're late. You're always late.

MARTY: The buses are often late, too, Mrs. Golo.

MRS. GOLO: Look, Jenny takes the bus, and she's always on time.

MARTY: But she's never early. Right, Mrs. Golo?

MRS. GOLO: Sit down and be quiet.

ADVERBS OF FREQUENCY WITH VERB "TO BE"

She's always on time.

_____ usually _____.

_____ often _____.

_____ sometimes _____.

_____ seldom _____.

_____ never _____.

PRACTICE • Add **always, usually, often, sometimes, seldom,** or **never** to the sentences.

Marty is on time. (never)
Marty is never on time.

The buses are late. (often)
The buses are often late.

1. Jenny is on time. (always)
2. Mr. Brown is early. (sometimes)
3. Nancy is in a hurry. (usually)
4. Barney is worried. (never)
5. Paris is beautiful. (always)
6. Bankers are poor. (seldom)
7. Antique clocks are expensive. (usually)
8. Old books are interesting. (often)
9. Police officers are friendly. (sometimes)
10. Teachers are rich. (seldom)
11. Movie stars are handsome. (usually)
12. Fenwick is hungry. (always)

FREE RESPONSE

A: Are you often late?
B: Yes, I am. OR **No, I'm never late. I'm always on time.**

1. Are you always happy?
2. Are you ever sad?
3. Are you often hungry?
4. Are you often thirsty?
5. Are you usually on time?
6. Are you ever late?
7. Are your friends sometimes late?
8. Are you often in a hurry?
9. Are you usually busy?
10. Are you often tired?
11. Are you ever worried?
12. Are you ever afraid?

Jack Grubb works at night. He has a part-time job downtown. Jack isn't married and he doesn't have a family. He lives alone in a small apartment on Bond Street. Jack has an easy life; he has a lot of free time and no responsibilities. He spends most of his free time at the park across the street from his apartment. He likes the park because there are always a lot of people there. Jack often gets bored when he's alone in his apartment. But he never feels bored or lonely when he's at the park.

Jack goes to the park in the afternoon. He usually sits on a bench and reads the newspaper. Sometimes he meets interesting people in the park. They have conversations about all kinds of things, but most of the time they talk about sports and politics. Jack knows a lot about these subjects. He doesn't have a college education, but he's an intelligent man. He reads two or three books a week. At the moment, Jack isn't reading or talking. He's feeding the pigeons. He's giving them bread crumbs. Jack always has a good time in the park.

STORY QUESTIONS

1. Does Jack work during the day?
2. Is he a family man?
3. Where does he live?
4. Does he have an easy life? Why?
5. Where does he spend his free time?
6. Why does Jack like the park?
7. What does he do there?
8. Does he ever meet interesting people in the park?
9. What do they talk about?
10. Does Jack like to read?
11. Is he reading or talking at the moment?
12. What's he doing?
13. Do you think Jack enjoys life? Why or why not?

FREE RESPONSE

1. Where do you live?
2. Is there a park near your home? What's it like?
3. How often do you go to the park?
4. How do you spend your free time?
5. Do you ever feel bored?
6. Where do you meet people?
7. What do you talk about with your friends?
8. Do you ever write to your friends?
9. Do you read many books? magazines?
10. What's your favorite subject?

WRITTEN EXERCISE • *Complete the sentences using the affirmative or negative form of the verb.*

Anne and Barbara are secretaries. They (work) ____*work*____ at the bank.

Barbara takes the bus to work. She (drive) _*doesn't drive*_ a car.

1. Tino is a happy man. He (have) _____ a wonderful life.

2. The Brown family isn't rich. They (live) _____ in a big house.

3. Jimmy likes all sports. He (play) _____ football, basketball, and baseball.

4. The Golos never listen to the Rolling Stones. They (like) _____ rock music.

5. They enjoy classical music. They (listen to) _____ Mozart and Beethoven.

6. Marty is a bad student. He (do) _____ his homework.

7. I don't know the time. I (have) _____ a watch.

8. Those women are doctors. They (work) _____ in a hospital.

9. Gloria is very intelligent. She (read) _____ a lot of books.

Listen and repeat.

PAIR WORK • *Ask and answer questions about the pictures on page 14.*

> 1. A: **Does Barney often shave?**
>   B: **No, he seldom shaves.**
>
> 2. A: **Does Mr. Bascomb often drink coffee?**
>   B: **Yes, he usually drinks coffee.**

3. Does Anne often sing in the shower?
4. Does Jack ever cut the grass?
5. Do Jenny and Lisa ever wear jeans?
6. Does Barbara usually take the bus to work?
7. Does Dr. Pasto often play the piano?
8. Do Jimmy and Linda ever go to the beach?

READING: GLORIA'S MORNING ROUTINE

Every morning Gloria Cole gets up at seven o'clock. She brushes her teeth, takes a shower, and gets dressed. Then she goes to the kitchen and makes breakfast. She usually has orange juice and cereal for breakfast. After breakfast, she reads the newspaper. At eight o'clock she leaves the house and goes to work.

PAIR WORK • *Ask and answer questions about Gloria's morning routine.*

1. When does Gloria get up?
2. Does she take a bath or a shower?
3. What does she have for breakfast?
4. Does she read the newspaper?
5. When does she leave the house?
6. Where does she go?

GROUP WORK • *Talk about your morning routine. Take turns asking questions like these:*

When do you get up? What do you have for breakfast? and so on.

COMPOSITION • *Write about your morning routine. What do you normally do from the time you get up until you leave the house?*

Start like this: *Every morning I get up at* _____

Listen and practice.

ROLE PLAY • *Imagine you're at a party. Introduce yourself to the people around you. Ask questions like "Where are you from?" and "What do you do?"*

GRAMMAR SUMMARY

SIMPLE PRESENT Affirmative

He She	lives	
I You We They	live	in New York.

Negative

He She	doesn't (does not)	
I You We They	don't (do not)	live in New York.

Interrogative

Does	he she	
Do	I you we they	live in New York?

Short Answers

Yes,	he she	does.	No,	he she	doesn't.
	I you we they	do.		I you we they	don't.

Questions with WHO, WHAT, WHERE, WHEN

Who lives in that house? What does he do?	Mr. Bascomb. He's a banker.
Where do those women work? When do they have lunch?	At the post office. At twelve o'clock.

ADVERBS OF FREQUENCY: Action Verbs

They	always usually often sometimes seldom never	come	early. late. on time.

ADVERBS OF FREQUENCY: To Be

They're	always usually often sometimes seldom never	early. late. on time.

Interrogative

Do they	ever	take the bus?

Negative

They	never	take the bus.

Chapter 2

TOPICS

Food and drinks

Friends

Clothes

GRAMMAR

Simple present vs. present continuous

"Would like"

Possessive pronouns

FUNCTIONS

Offering food

Ordering in a restaurant

Talking about feelings

1

2

1. *Talk about the pictures.*
2. *Listen to the stories.*
3. *Answer the story questions.*

READING

1 Jimmy Brown is a student in high school. He likes his classes and gets good grades. Jimmy usually studies with his friends in the school library. He often helps them with their lessons. After school they sometimes go to the park and play football. Right now Jimmy is watching television.

1. Where does Jimmy study?
2. Is he studying now?
3. Does Jimmy help his friends with their lessons?
4. Is he helping them now?
5. Where does Jimmy go after school?
6. Is he going there now?
7. What's he doing?

2 Tino Martinoli works every day at his father's restaurant. He's very friendly and smiles at all the customers. Tino's friends often come and see him at the restaurant. They usually talk about sports. At the moment Tino is playing tennis with Barbara and he's losing.

1. What does Tino do every day?
2. Is he working now?
3. What does Tino talk about with his friends?
4. Is he talking with them now?
5. What's he doing?
6. Is he smiling?
7. Why not?

PRESENT CONTINUOUS
She's taking a shower.
_____ making breakfast.
_____ drinking coffee.
_____ reading the newspaper.

SIMPLE PRESENT
She takes a shower every morning.
_____ makes breakfast _____.
_____ drinks coffee _____.
_____ reads the newspaper _____.

PRACTICE • *Change the sentences from the present continuous to the simple present.*

Jimmy is watching television. (every day)
He watches television every day.

Barbara and Tino are playing tennis. (every week)
They play tennis every week.

1. Anne is taking a shower. (every morning)
2. Mr. and Mrs. Golo are listening to the radio. (every day)
3. Jack is going to the park. (every afternoon)
4. Nancy is cleaning the windows. (every week)
5. Sam and Mabel are painting their house. (every year)
6. Maria is writing a letter to her mother. (every month)
7. Fred and Barney are playing cards. (every day)
8. Peter is reading the newspaper. (every morning)
9. Mr. and Mrs. Farley are going to church. (every Sunday)

Listen and practice.

TINO: You're playing well today, Barbara.

BARBARA: I always play well, Tino.

TINO: But you don't always win.

BARBARA: I'm winning today.

TINO: You're just lucky.

BARBARA: That's right, Tino. I'm lucky today.

MRS. BASCOMB: What are you making, John?

MR. BASCOMB: Some tea.

MRS. BASCOMB: That's unusual.

MR. BASCOMB: Yes, I usually make coffee, but not today. Today I'm making tea.

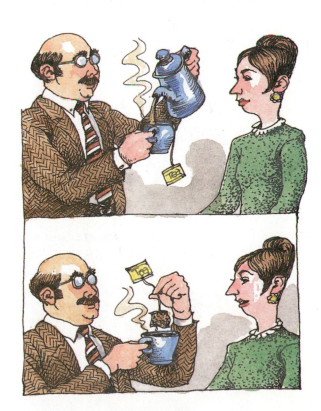

1. Mr. Bascomb/make coffee?

A: **Does Mr. Bascomb usually make coffee?**
B: **Yes, but not today. Today he's making tea.**

2. Barbara and Tino/play tennis in the park?

A: **Do Barbara and Tino play tennis in the park?**
B: **Yes, but not today. Today they're playing tennis at the Racquet Club.**

3. Gloria/get up at seven o'clock?

4. Mr. and Mrs. Farley/take the bus to work?

5. Fred and Barney/eat at Mom's?

6. Fred/have a sandwich for lunch?

7. Anne/go home after work?

8. Jenny and Marty/study at home?

Listen and practice.

PAIR WORK • *Have similar conversations.*

A: Hi, _____. Nice to see you.

B: Hi, _____.

A: Come in. Make yourself at home.

B: Thank you.

A: Would you like something to drink/eat?

B: Yes, please. I'd like some_____.
OR   No, thanks. I'm not thirsty/hungry.

CONVERSATION

Listen and practice.

WAITER: Good evening. Are you ready to order?

SUZI: Yes. I'd like some tomato soup.

WAITER: And for the main course?

SUZI: I'd like roast beef.

WAITER: Yes, ma'am. Anything to drink?

SUZI: A cup of coffee, please.

WAITER: Is that all?

SUZI: Yes, thank you.

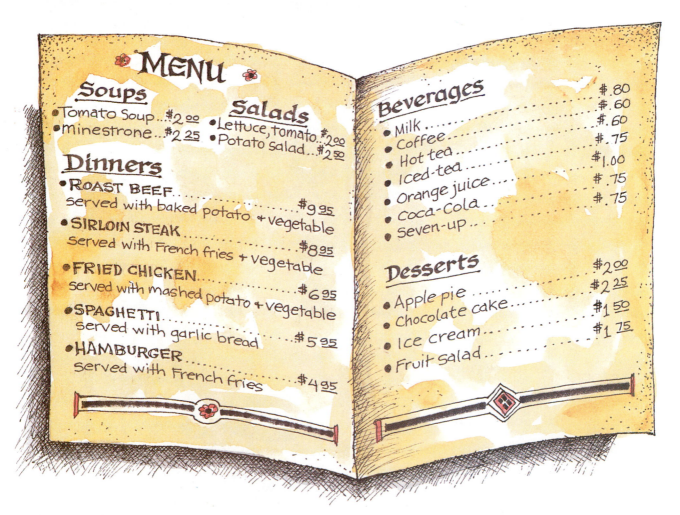

ROLE PLAY • *Practice ordering from the menu. After the first conversation, exchange roles.*

Listen and repeat.

POSSESSIVE ADJECTIVES	POSSESSIVE PRONOUNS
my	mine
your	yours
his	his
her	hers
our	ours
their	theirs

PAIR WORK • *Ask and answer questions.*

Barney Field works for the Speedy Cab Company. He's an excellent driver and knows the city well. Barney enjoys his work because he meets interesting people on the job. He's very friendly and always talks with his passengers. Sometimes he tells them amusing stories about his experiences as a taxi driver. Barney often meets foreign visitors, and he gives them useful information about the city. He knows all the good restaurants, hotels and nightclubs.

Barney takes good care of his car. He stops at Nick's garage every day, but he seldom buys any gas there. It's very hot this afternoon, and Nick is putting water in the radiator. One of his employees is cleaning the windows and the other is putting air in the tires. Barney is drinking a cup of coffee and having a short conversation with Nick.

"My garage is a long way from the center of town," says Nick. "Why do you always bring your car here?"

"Because you're my friend," says Barney. "And I never forget my friends."

STORY QUESTIONS

1. What company does Barney work for?
2. Why does he enjoy his work?
3. Where does Barney go every day?
4. Does he often buy gas there?
5. What's Nick doing at this moment?
6. What are his employees doing?
7. What's Barney doing?
8. Is Nick's garage near the center of town?
9. Why does Barney always take his car there?
10. Do you think Nick is happy to have a friend like Barney? Why or why not?

PRACTICE • *Combine the sentences with **because**.*

Barney enjoys his work. It's interesting.
Barney enjoys his work because it's interesting.

1. He's thirsty. It's hot today.
2. Mabel is cleaning the kitchen. It's dirty.
3. People like Dr. Pasto. He's friendly.
4. Mr. Bascomb is taking his umbrella. It's raining.
5. Maria is smiling. She's happy.
6. Otis doesn't eat meat. He's a vegetarian.
7. Linda isn't eating her dinner. She isn't hungry.
8. Barbara takes the bus to work. She doesn't have a car.
9. Peter isn't working today. He's sick.

WRITTEN EXERCISE • *Complete the sentences using possessive adjectives and possessive pronouns.*

Mr. and Mrs. Golo are cleaning _____*their*_____ house.

Give me that magazine! It's _____*mine*_____.

1. Mr. Bascomb is talking to_____ secretary.

2. What does she have in_____ handbag?

3. That dictionary belongs to us. It's_____.

4. Take this book to Jimmy and Linda. It's_____.

5. I have _____ classes in the morning and Linda has _____ in the afternoon.

6. Albert says those cards are _____.

7. Don't take that pen! It isn't _____.

8. You have_____ birthday in July and I have _____ in August.

9. We're waiting for _____ friends. They're coming in _____ car.

PAIR WORK • *Ask and answer questions.*

1. A: **What's Barney doing?**
   B: **He's shining his shoes.**
   He shines his shoes once a week.

2. A: **What are Mr. and Mrs. Golo doing?**
   B: **They're making the bed.**
   They make the bed every morning.

1. Barney/shoes/once a week

2. Mr. and Mrs. Golo/bed/every morning

3. Maria/teeth/twice a day

4. The Bascombs/newspaper/every morning

5. Robert/girlfriend/all the time

6. Sam and Mabel/house/once a year

7. Jack/pigeons/every day

8. Barbara and Tino/tennis/every Sunday

Listen and repeat.

1. Anne is nervous.

2. Gloria is excited.

3. Johnnie is embarrassed.

4. Mr. Farley is worried.

5. Mrs. Golo is angry.

6. Mrs. Bascomb is disappointed.

7. Fred and Barney are happy.

8. Marty is sad.

9. Mr. and Mrs. Farley are scared.

PAIR WORK • *Ask and answer questions about the pictures.*

> 1. Anne
> A: **Why is Anne nervous?**
> B: **Because Mr. Bascomb is watching her.**

PAIR WORK I • *Take turns asking questions about feelings.*

> A: **How do you feel when you go the dentist?**
> B: **I feel nervous.** OR **I'm scared.**

1. . . . when someone brings you flowers?
2. . . . when people don't listen to you?
3. . . . when a good friend moves to another city?
4. . . . when the teacher asks you a question and you don't know the answer?
5. . . . when you hear beautiful music?
6. . . . when your friends forget your birthday?
7. . . . when you take a test?
8. . . . when you see a rat?
9. . . . when your team wins a big game?
10. . . . when your team loses a big game?

READING • GOOD FRIENDS

Fred and Barney are good friends. They both live in Wickam City, and they see each other every day. They like to play cards, go to football games, and eat at Mom's Cafe. Fred and Barney talk about everything——movies, sports, politics, even their personal problems. And because they're good friends, they always help each other. For example, if Fred doesn't have money to take the bus, Barney gives him a free ride in his taxi. Fred thinks he's lucky to have a friend like Barney, and Barney feels the same way about Fred.

PAIR WORK 2 • *Ask and answer questions about Fred and Barney.*

1. Where do Fred and Barney live?
2. How often do they see each other?
3. What kind of things do they do together?
4. How old are Fred and Barney?
5. What do they talk about?
6. Why is Fred lucky to have a friend like Barney?

GROUP WORK • *Talk about your good friends. Take turns asking questions.*

1. What's your friend's name?
2. Where does he or she live?
3. What does he or she do?
4. What's he or she like?
5. How often do you see each other?
6. What do you do together?
7. What do you talk about?
8. Do you help each other? How?

COMPOSITION • *Write about a good friend of yours.*

Start like this: *I have a good friend named*

Listen and repeat.

Barbara wears a swimsuit when she goes to the beach.

Jimmy wears tennis shoes when he plays basketball.

Maria wears high heels on special occasions.

Otis wears shorts on hot days.

Anne wears gloves when it's cold.

Peter wears a suit when he goes to work.

PRACTICE • *Can you name these articles of clothing?*

PAIR WORK • *Ask and answer questions about the articles of clothing.*

1. tie
A: **When do you wear a tie?**
B: **I wear a tie when I go to work.** OR **I never wear a tie.**

GRAMMAR SUMMARY

PRESENT SIMPLE

He	always usually often sometimes seldom	goes to the movies.

PRESENT CONTINUOUS

Is he going to the movies now?

WOULD LIKE

Would you like something to drink?	Yes, I would.	No, I wouldn't.

What would you like?	I'd like some lemonade.

POSSESSIVE ADJECTIVES

It's	my your our their his her	house.

POSSESSIVE PRONOUNS

It's	mine. yours. ours. theirs. his. hers.

Chapter 3

Listen and read.

1

Mrs. Brown is a good cook. She can make spaghetti, chocolate cake, banana bread, and fried chicken.

2

Mr. Brown has a big appetite. He can eat a whole chicken, a chocolate cake, three hamburgers, and five hot dogs.

3

Jimmy is very athletic. He can play basketball, football, baseball, and tennis.

4

Nancy is very intelligent. She can speak French, German, Spanish, and English.

CAN: Affirmative

Jimmy can play tennis.	They can play the piano.
He _____.	You _____.
Linda_____.	We _____.
She _____.	I _____.

FREE RESPONSE 1

1. What languages can you speak?
2. What languages can your parents speak?
3. What sports can you play?
4. What musical instruments can you play?
5. What songs can you sing?
6. What dances can you do?
7. What games can you play?
8. What dishes can you make?

checkers   chess

violin   flute
trumpet   guitar   drums   piano   cards

PRACTICE • *Listen and repeat.*

Anne can play the guitar, but she can't play the trumpet.

Fred and Barney can swim, but they can't ski.

FREE RESPONSE 2

What are some things you can and can't do? Talk about musical instruments, sports, games, languages, or anything you want.

I can sing, but I can't dance.

I can play tennis, but I can't play golf.

Listen and practice.

TINO: What kind of movies do you like, Barbara?

BARBARA: I like French movies.

TINO: Can you speak French?

BARBARA: No, but I can understand it.

SAM BROWN: Can you make a banana cake today?

MABEL BROWN: No, I can't.

SAM BROWN: Why not?

MABEL BROWN: I don't have any bananas.

1. A: **Can you speak French?**
   B: **Yes, I can.** OR **No, I can't.**

2. _____ play the violin?

3. _____ repair a car?

4. _____ make pizza?

5. _____ type?

6. _____ ride a bike?

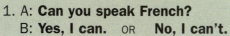

7. _____ drive a truck?

8. _____ dance?

9. _____ play basketball?

1

2

1. Talk about the pictures.
2. Listen to the stories.
3. Answer the story questions.

READING

1 It's a beautiful summer day. Tino wants to go to the park and play tennis. But he can't leave the restaurant. He has to stay and help his father. There are a lot of customers today, and Tino has to take their orders.

1. What kind of day is it?
2. What does Tino want to do?
3. Why can't he go to the park?
4. Who does he have to help?
5. Are there many customers today?
6. Does Tino have to take their orders?

2 There's a good movie playing at the Rex Cinema today. It's a western with Tex Laredo called *The Last Texan*. Linda wants to go and see it. But first she has to clean the kitchen and wash the dishes. Then she can go to the movies.

1. What movie is playing at the Rex Cinema?
2. Who's in it?
3. What does Linda want to do?
4. What does she have to do first?
5. What does Jimmy have to do today?

PAIR WORK • *Ask and answer questions about the pictures.*

1. A: **Why can't Tino play tennis today?**
   B: **Because he has to help his father.**

2. A: **Why can't Elmer and Sarah watch TV now?**
   B: **Because they have to feed the chickens.**

3. Why can't Mrs. Golo read the newspaper now?

4. Why can't Sam and Mabel see their friends today?

5. Why can't Mr. Bascomb go home now?

6. Why can't Marty and Jenny go to the movies?

7. Why can't Gloria talk on the phone now?

8. Why can't the Farleys go to the park today?

9. Why can't Peter go out with his girlfriend?

Listen and practice.

MR. BASCOMB: What are you looking at?

MRS. BASCOMB: The sky. It's getting cloudy.

MR. BASCOMB: Do you think it's going to rain?

MRS. BASCOMB: I hope not. I have to go to the store.

MR. BASCOMB: Can't you go tomorrow?

MRS. BASCOMB: No, I have to go now. I have to get some food for dinner.

MR. BASCOMB: Don't worry about dinner. We can go to a restaurant tonight.

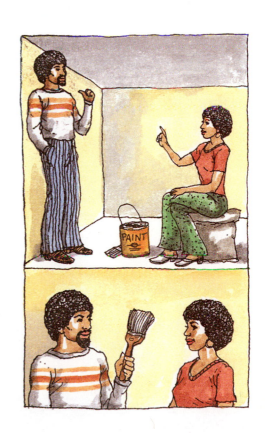

OTIS: Can you go out today, Gloria?

GLORIA: I don't think so, Otis. I have to paint this room.

OTIS: Do you have to do it now?

GLORIA: I'm afraid so. I'm expecting some guests this weekend.

OTIS: I can help you. I'm pretty good with a brush.

GLORIA: That's nice of you. We can go out afterwards.

• *Ask and answer questions.*

1. A: **Does Mrs. Bascomb have to make dinner tonight?**
   B: **No, she doesn't.**
   A: **Why not?**
   B: **Because she's going to a restaurant.**

2. A: **Do Anne and Barbara have to be nice to Mr. Bascomb?**
   B: **Yes, they do.**
   A: **Why?**
   B: **Because he's the boss.**

3. Does Dr. Pasto have to water the plants today?

4. Does Maria have to go to the market?

5. Do Jimmy and Linda have to be quiet?

6. Does Peter have to get some gas soon?

7. Do these men have to hurry?

8. Do these men have to pay for their food?

It's Wednesday night at the Martinoli Restaurant. Tino is talking with Mr. and Mrs. Hamby. They're regular customers at the restaurant. Mr. Hamby wants a big plate of spaghetti with meat sauce. For dessert he wants some Italian ice cream. His wife can't have spaghetti or ice cream. She has to watch her weight. Mrs. Hamby is ordering a bowl of vegetable soup for dinner. She doesn't want any dessert.

"There's no vegetable soup," says Tino. "But I can bring you some chicken soup."

"Wonderful," says Mrs. Hamby. "I love chicken soup."

"This is a fine restaurant," says Mr. Hamby. "Except for one thing."

"What's that?" says Tino.

"There's no music."

"You need some Italian music," says Mrs. Hamby. "And some pictures of Italy on the wall."

"That's a good idea," says Tino. "I have some pictures of Venice at home. I can use them."

"Wonderful," says Mrs. Hamby. "I love Venice."

STORY QUESTIONS

1. What night is it?
2. What's Tino doing?
3. Do the Hambys often go to the Martinoli Restaurant?
4. What does Mr. Hamby want for dinner?
5. What does Mrs. Hamby want?
6. Does she want any dessert? Why not?
7. What is Mr. Hamby's opinion of the Martinoli Restaurant?
8. What does the restaurant need?

CONVERSATION

Listen and practice.

PAIR WORK • *Have similar conversations. Invite your partner to a movie, to the park, or anywhere.*

A: Hi, _____. Can you _____ today?

B: No, I can't. I have to _____.

1. _____ my clothes.

2. _____ the market.

3. _____ my homework.

4. _____ some letters.

5. _____ my apartment.

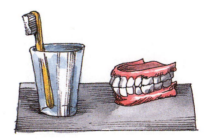

6. _____ the dentist.

Listen and practice.

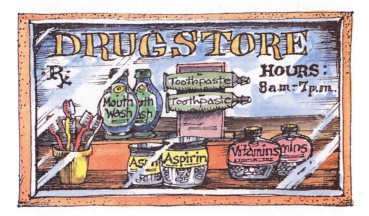

You need some aspirin. It's 6:30 p.m.

A: Where can I get some aspirin?

B: At the drugstore.

A: Is it still open?

B: Yes, it's open until seven.

You need a ruler. It's 5:45 p.m.

A: Where can I get a ruler?

B: At the stationery store.

A: Is it still open?

B: No, it closes at five-thirty.

You need a lock. It's 8:30 a.m.

A: Where can I get a lock?

B: At the hardware store.

A: Is it open now?

B: No, it opens at nine.

PAIR WORK • *Have similar conversations.*

1. You need some pencils. It's 8:45 a.m.
2. You need a hammer. It's 6:20 p.m.
3. You need some toothpaste. It's 6:40 p.m.
4. You need a paintbrush. It's 8:30 a.m.
5. You need some vitamins. It's 9:00 a.m.
6. You need a pen. It's 5:10 p.m.
7. You need some mouthwash. It's 7:30 p.m.
8. You need some nails. It's 9:15 a.m.
9. You need a notebook. It's 6:00 p.m.
10. You need a toothbrush. It's 6:30 p.m.
11. You need some envelopes. It's 5:45 p.m.
12. You need some paint. It's 8:50 a.m.

Listen and repeat.

FREE RESPONSE • *Tell why you use or don't use each kind of transportation. Use these adjectives:* **cheap, expensive, fast, slow, safe, dangerous, comfortable, uncomfortable.**

1. metro
   I take the metro because it's fast and cheap.
   OR   **I don't take the metro because it's crowded and uncomfortable.**
   OR   **I don't take the metro because we don't have one in our city.**

1. metro (subway)   2. bus   3. taxi

FREE RESPONSE

1. Do you have good public transportation in your city?
2. How often do you take the bus? Are the buses usually on time?
3. Does your city have a metro? Do you feel safe when you take the metro?
4. Do you ever take a taxi? What do taxi drivers have to know?
5. Are taxis expensive in your city? How much is a taxi ride to the airport?
6. What are the most important streets in your city?
7. Why are there so many cars in the street between five and six p.m.?
8. Do you think most people are good drivers? Do you know any dangerous drivers?

READING

Mom's Cafe is a very popular place to eat. Everyone goes there because the food is delicious and the prices are reasonable. You can have a big hamburger and French fries at Mom's for only three dollars. And the service is excellent. Mom is very friendly with all her customers; she has a smile for everyone. The only problem with Mom's Cafe is that it's too popular. It often gets very crowded and there's no place to sit.

PAIR WORK • *Ask and answer questions about Mom's Cafe.*

1. Why is Mom's Cafe so popular?
2. What can you get for three dollars?
3. How is the service?
4. Is Mom nice to her customers?
5. Can you name two of her regular customers?
6. What is the only problem with Mom's Cafe?

GROUP WORK • *Talk about your favorite places to eat. Take turns asking questions.*

1. Where is your favorite place to eat?
2. Why do you like it?
3. What kind of food do they serve?
4. Is it expensive?
5. When is it open?
6. Who goes there?
7. Is it a good place for conversation?
8. Do they have music?
9. Do you often go there with your friends?
10. Do you ever meet new people there?

COMPOSITION • *Write about your favorite place to eat. Why do you go there?*

GRAMMAR SUMMARY

CAN Affirmative

He She I You We They	can	swim.

Negative

He She I You We They	can't (cannot)	swim.

Interrogative

Can	he she I you we they	swim?

Short Answers

Yes,	he she I you we they	can.	No,	he she I you we they	can't.

HAVE TO Affirmative

He She	has to	get up early. make breakfast. go to the market.
I You We They	have to	

Negative

He She	doesn't (does not)	have to	get up early. make breakfast. go to the market.
I You We They	don't (do not)		

Interrogative

Does	he she	have to	get up early? make breakfast? go to the market?
Do	I you we they		

Short Answers

Yes,	he she	does.	No,	he she	doesn't.
	I you we they	do.		I you we they	don't.

Review Chapter

TOPICS
Locations, where to buy things
Occupations
Daily routines
Clothes

GRAMMAR
Review

FUNCTIONS
Asking about and indicating locations
Borrowing
Taking a bus
Giving explanations
Buying clothes

Listen and practice.

STORY QUESTIONS

1. Where are Peter and Maria?
2. What kind of day is it?
3. What does Peter smell?
4. How much time do they have before the movie starts?
5. What can Maria see in the pond?
6. Are there any fish in Marty's bucket?
7. What does Peter say about a good fisherman?
8. Why is Marty happy to give Peter his fishing pole and worms?
9. What does the sign say?
10. Why can't Peter read the sign?
11. What does the officer say to Peter?
12. Why is the officer surprised that Peter and Maria are going to a movie?

PAIR WORK I • *Ask and answer questions.*

> at the library
> A: **What can you do at the library?**
> B: **You can read, study, get information, borrow books, and so on.**

1. at the park
2. at the zoo
3. at the beach
4. at a party
5. downtown
6. at home

PAIR WORK 2 • *Ask and answer questions.*

> with lemons, water, and sugar
> A: **What can you do with lemons, water, and sugar?**
> B: **You can make lemonade.**

1. with ice, fruit, and cream
2. with bread, ham, and cheese
3. with some wood, a hammer, and nails
4. with a pen and paper
5. with a paintbrush and some paint
6. with $5.00; with $50.00; with $5,000.00

FREE RESPONSE

1. How do you like your English class?
2. Where do you go after class?
3. How often do you see your friends? Where do you meet? What do you do?
4. What do you do when a friend asks you for money? What about a stranger?
5. What do you do when you're tired? hungry? sick? bored? lonely?
6. Do you often help other people? How?
7. Do you have any friends from foreign countries? What language(s) do they speak?
8. How often do you write letters? Who do you write to?
9. Is there someone special in your life? Who is it? What do you like about this person?
10. Describe your life. Is it easy? hard? sad? wonderful?

PAIR WORK 1 • *Ask and answer questions using the verbs listed below. Begin your questions with* **what, when,** *or* **where.**

> watch
> A: **What TV programs do you watch?**
> B: **I watch sports and the news.**
>
> study
> A: **Where do you study?**
> B: **I study at the library.**

1. live	4. get up	7. study
2. work	5. eat	8. watch
3. play	6. go	9. listen to

PRACTICE • *Change the sentences using* **have** *and* **any** *or* **one.**

> Peter needs some stamps.
> **He doesn't have any.**
>
> They need a car.
> **They don't have one.**

1. Linda needs some toothpaste.
2. I need some shampoo.
3. Jack needs an umbrella.
4. He needs some tennis shoes.
5. We need a dictionary.
6. You need some large towels.
7. Maria needs a teapot.
8. She needs some sugar.
9. Wickam City needs a good hotel.

PAIR WORK 2 • *Ask and answer questions using the verb* **to need.**

> babies
> A: **What do babies need?**
> B: **They need milk.**

1. flowers	4. a tired person	7. your family
2. cars	5. a sick person	8. this school
3. tires	6. you	9. this town

CONVERSATION

Look at the picture on page 55. Listen and practice.

A: Where can I get some detergent?
B: At the market.

A: Is there a market nearby?
B: Yes, there's one on Franklin Avenue, across from the church.

A: Where can I get a sandwich?
B: At Mom's Cafe.

A: Where is Mom's Cafe?
B: It's on Main Street, between the bank and the theater.

PAIR WORK 3 • *Have similar conversations.*

1. some roses
2. some stamps
3. a cup of coffee
4. a map of the city
5. some aspirin
6. an umbrella
7. some paper plates
8. a dictionary
9. some traveler's checks
10. a haircut

map   traveler's checks

I drive people everywhere.   I sell cars.   I repair cars.
I take care of sick people.   I make movies.   I fly airplanes.
I play basketball.   I sing.   I paint pictures.

1. Larry Sharp

2. Nick Vitakis

3. Barney Field

4. Bonita Cantata

5. Billy Chambers

6. Nancy Paine

7. Otis Jackson

8. Maria Miranda

9. Franco Fellini

PAIR WORK • *Ask and answer questions about the people on page 56.*

1. Larry Sharp
A: **What does Larry Sharp do?**
B: **He's a car dealer. He sells cars.**

ROLE PLAY • *Choose one of the occupations on page 56. Interview each other about your "new" occupation.*

1. What do you do?
2. Do you work hard?
3. How much do you make?
4. Do you like your job?
5. What are the good things about it?
6. What are the bad things?

WRITTEN EXERCISE • *Complete the sentences using possessive adjectives and possessive pronouns.*

I'm writing a letter to _my_ sister.

Don't take that pen. It isn't _yours_ .

1. I wash _____ car every week. How often do you wash _____?

2. What do the Browns have in _____ garage?

3. We clean _____ apartment once a week. They clean _____ once a month.

4. Albert is asking Linda for _____ telephone number.

5. We're taking the computer because it's _____.

6. Mr. Bascomb says those envelopes are _____. Give them to him.

7. I never forget _____ birthday. Why do you always forget _____?

8. Please give this book to Anne. It's _____.

9. Jimmy always takes _____ notebook when he goes to school.

PRACTICE • *Change the sentences using object pronouns.*

Otis is showing some paintings <u>to Dr. Pasto</u>.
He is showing <u>him</u> some paintings.

1. Peter is taking some flowers <u>to Maria.</u>
2. Barbara is showing a photograph <u>to Tino.</u>
3. Sam is getting a computer <u>for Jimmy and Linda.</u>
4. Jimmy is writing a letter <u>to his girlfriend.</u>
5. Nancy is giving a dictionary <u>to Barney.</u>
6. Maria is buying a television <u>for her parents.</u>
7. I'm taking these books <u>to my sister.</u>
8. Gloria is making cookies <u>for Otis.</u>
9. Albert is showing his camera <u>to the Browns.</u>

Listen and practice.

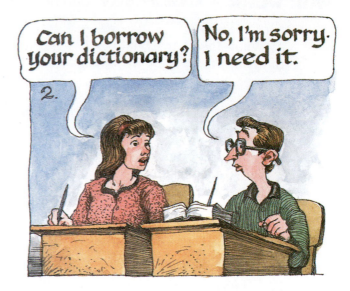

PRACTICE • *Can you name these items?*

PAIR WORK • *Ask if you can borrow these items.*

Possible affirmative answers.	Possible negative answers.
Yes or yeah.	No.
Sure.	I'm sorry.
OK.	Not today.
Of course.	I need it/them.
No problem.	I don't have one/any.

CARTOON STORY

  Listen and practice.

STORY QUESTIONS

1. Where is Linda going?
2. Which bus goes downtown?
3. How much is the bus fare?
4. Describe the bus driver.
5. Talk about the passengers. What are they doing?
6. Does Linda get off on Pine Street?
7. Why do you think Linda is going downtown?
8. How often do you go downtown?
9. What are some of your favorite destinations?

PAIR WORK • *You're at the bus stop and you need some information. Get the information from the person next to you.*

A: Excuse me. Which bus goes ____?

B: _____ .

A: How much is the fare?

B: _____ .

A: Thank you.

B: You're welcome.

PAIR WORK • *Ask and answer questions about the pictures.*

1. Mr. Farley
A: **Why is Mr. Farley unhappy?**
B: **He's unhappy because his wife isn't ready.**

1. Mr. Farley

2. Mr. and Mrs. Farley

3. Gina

4. Tino and Barbara

5. Mrs. Bascomb

6. Betty and Louise

7. Barney

8. Joe

Listen and practice.

PAIR WORK • *Have similar conversations. Choose one article of clothing you would like to buy.*

A: Can I help you?

B: Yes. I want to get a _____.

A: The _____ are over here. What size?

B: _____.

A: What color would you like?

B: I'd like _____.

A: Here.

B: It's very nice. How much?

A: _____ dollars.

B: Oh, that's too expensive.
    OR   All right.

Sizes: large, medium, small   Colors: red, blue, yellow, green, brown, gray, black

Talk about the people in the pictures. What do these people do every day?

1. Nancy/7:15 coffee and toast motorcycle pilot/flies airplanes

Nancy gets up at seven-fifteen. She has coffee and toast for breakfast. After breakfast, she rides her motorcycle to work. Nancy is a pilot. She flies airplanes.

2. Nick/7:30 coffee and doughnuts car mechanic/repairs cars

3. Mrs. Farley/6:45 orange juice and cereal bus receptionist/ answers the phone

4. Mr. Wong/7:00 coffee and eggs motorcycle photographer/ takes pictures

PAIR WORK 1 • *Ask and answer questions about the daily routines of the people on page 62. When do they get up? What do they have for breakfast? How do they go to work? and so on.*

PAIR WORK 2 • *Ask and answer questions.*

> go to the market
> A: **How often do you go to the market?**
> B: **I go to the market every day/twice a week, and so on.** OR **I never go to the market.**

1. take a shower
2. wash your hair
3. shine your shoes
4. change your socks
5. clean your room
6. make dinner
7. wash the dishes
8. drink coffee/tea
9. brush your teeth
10. go to the dentist/doctor
11. get a haircut
12. exercise/play a sport

WRITTEN EXERCISE • *Complete the sentences using the simple present or the present continuous.*

> Barbara always _takes_ the bus to work. (take)
>
> She _is waiting_ at the bus stop right now. (wait)

1. Nick is busy today. He _____ at the garage. (work)

2. The garage _____ at 8 a.m. (open) It _____ at 6 p.m. (close)

3. Nick _____ his job. (like) He _____ it's interesting. (think)

4. Come on. Our friends _____ for us. (wait)

5. Take your umbrella. It _____. (rain)

6. Mr. Bascomb is in the kitchen. He _____ breakfast. (make)

7. He usually _____ coffee with his breakfast. (drink)

8. He _____ his coffee with cream and sugar. (like)

9. Mrs. Bascomb is sitting in the living room. She _____ a letter. (write)

10. Look at the cat! It _____ on the sofa. (sleep)

FREE RESPONSE

1. How often do you go to parties? What kind of parties do you like?
2. Who makes dinner at your home? What time do you have dinner?
3. Do you have interesting conversations at dinner? What do you talk about?
4. Do you often go out on the weekend? Where do you go? What do you do?
5. Do you need money to have a good time? What is your idea of a good time?
6. What kind of movies do you like? Are there any good movies playing now?
7. Do you like to shop? Where is a good place to shop for clothes?
8. What kind of clothes do you like to wear? What clothes do you need?

1. What is the color _____ your kitchen?
   a. for   c. in
   b. of   d. at

2. Do you have a television _____ your living room?
   a. on   c. to
   b. at   d. in

3. Mr. Grubb works _____ night.
   a. in   c. at
   b. during   d. for

4. There's a park across the street _____ the church.
   a. of   c. to
   b. from   d. for

5. Are there many trees _____ your street?
   a. at   c. on
   b. for   d. in

6. What do you want _____ lunch?
   a. for   c. to
   b. of   d. from

7. Call the waiter. Ask _____ for the menu.
   a. he   c. her
   b. him   d. them

8. Those aren't your books. Don't take _____.
   a. them   c. this
   b. they   d. it

9. Anne and I are busy. Don't talk to _____ now.
   a. her   c. us
   b. me   d. them

10. He's giving _____ some magazines.
    a. she   c. to her
    b. for her   d. her

11. _____ birthday is in July.
    a. My   c. Mine
    b. Me   d. They

12. The Browns are cleaning _____ house.
    a. they   c. there
    b. their   d. they're

13. That computer belongs to Barbara. It's _____.
    a. her   c. hers
    b. to her   d. she

14. I'm in a hurry. I'm _____ for work.
    a. early   c. late
    b. on time   d. ready

15. Anne isn't working today because she's _____.
    a. sick   c. bored
    b. at home   d. lonely

16. Can Tino _____ Italian?
    a. tell   c. talk
    b. say   d. speak

17. Your perfume _____ good.
    a. looks   c. feels
    b. smells   d. works

18. Mr. Poole doesn't have any friends. He's a _____ man.
    a. happy   c. lucky
    b. friendly   d. lonely

19. How does Maria go to work?
    a. By car.   c. In the morning.
    b. On time.   d. At the bus stop.

20. You can get stamps at the _____.
    a. gas station   c. post office
    b. library   d. bank

21. Oranges are my favorite _____.

    a. fruit   c. color
    b. vegetable   d. drink

22. Linda is _____. She wants a glass of water.

    a. busy   c. hungry
    b. tired   d. thirsty

23. Please wash the dishes. They're _____.

    a. clean   c. old
    b. new   d. dirty

24. _____ does Peter go to work? At nine o'clock.

    a. Why   c. When
    b. Where   d. How

25. _____ does he like his job? Because it's interesting.

    a. Why   c. When
    b. Where   d. How

26. Anne's coat is ten years old. She _____ a new coat.

    a. has   c. likes
    b. needs   d. wears

27. We always _____ at Mom's Cafe.

    a. are eating   c. eat
    b. eats   d. feed

28. I usually _____ dinner at six.

    a. has   c. am having
    b. having   d. have

29. The boys _____ football now.

    a. plays   c. are playing
    b. playing d. play

30. A good fisherman always _____ fish.

    a. catch   c. catching
    b. catches d. is catching

31. Sam is in the kitchen. He _____ coffee.

    a. is making c. make
    b. makes   d. making

32. Marty is a bad student. He _____ his homework.

    a. does not   c. doesn't do
    b. doesn't make d. don't do

33. Can you help me?

    a. No, I don't. c. No, I can.
    b. No, I'm not. d. No, I can't.

34. _____ some stamps in the desk.

    a. It has   c. There
    b. They're   d. There are

35. Albert is hungry. He wants _____ sandwich.

    a. a   c. some
    b. an   d. more

36. There's _____ bread on the table.

    a. a   c. some
    b. any   d. one

37. We don't have _____ butter.

    a. a   c. some
    b. any   d. one

38. Barbara is young _____ pretty.

    a. but   c. or
    b. because d. and

39. I'm not a very good athlete, _____ I like tennis.

    a. but   c. or
    b. because d. and

40. Johnnie is taking his umbrella _____ it's raining.

    a. but   c. or
    b. because d. and

41. Ula Hackey is _____.

    a. actress   c. an actress
    b. a actress   d. one actress

42. We _____ go to the movies, only once or twice a year.

    a. always   c. seldom
    b. often   d. never

43. I can't go out tonight. I'm very _____.

    a. free   c. lucky
    b. alone   d. busy

44. Would you like some coffee?

    a. No problem.
    b. Yes, please.
    c. I'm glad.
    d. That's too bad.

45. _____. We're late for the concert.

    a. Please hurry.
    b. Here we are.
    c. Thank you.
    d. Don't worry.

46. When are you leaving?

    a. Of course.
    b. Excuse me.
    c. Right now.
    d. That's right.

47. I'm American. What's your _____?

    a. composition   c. language
    b. personality   d. nationality

48. Where are you from?

    a. A long way.
    b. England.
    c. I'm fine.
    d. I'm a tourist.

49. Maria is a doctor. She takes care of _____ people.

    a. sick   c. strong
    b. well   d. boring

50. What is Maria like?

    a. She's American.
    b. She likes music and art.
    c. She would like a new car.
    d. She's smart, pretty, and friendly.

Chapter 5

TOPICS
Weather
Housework
Your street

GRAMMAR
Past tense with verb "to be"
Like to/want to

FUNCTIONS
Talking about the past
Describing the weather
Expressing likes and dislikes
Giving reasons and explanations

WEATHER REPORT

Today the weather is good all over Europe. It's sunny and warm.

Yesterday the weather was bad. It was rainy in Moscow, cold in Paris, windy in Rome, and cloudy in London.

 1. *Listen to the stories.*
2. *Answer the story questions.*

READING

1 Nancy Paine often travels to Europe. Yesterday she was in Moscow. She was unhappy because the weather was bad. It was rainy. Today Nancy is in London. The weather is good. It's sunny. Nancy is very happy.

1. Where was Nancy yesterday?
2. Why was she unhappy?
3. Where is Nancy today?
4. What's the weather like?

2 Mr. and Mrs. Golo are on vacation in Europe. Yesterday they were in Paris and the weather was terrible. It was very cold and damp. But today they're in Rome and the weather is fantastic. It's sunny and warm.

1. Where were Mr. and Mrs. Golo yesterday?
2. What was the weather like?
3. Where are Mr. and Mrs. Golo today?
4. What's the weather like?

WRITTEN EXERCISE • *Complete the sentences about the pictures using these adjectives:*
sad, thirsty, tired, cold, angry, busy, afraid, happy, hungry.

1. I was *tired*.

2. You were _____.

3. He was _____.

4. They were _____.

5. We were _____.

6. She was _____.

7. You were _____.

8. I was _____.

9. They were _____.

🔊 *Listen and practice.*

JOHNNIE: Welcome back, Peter. How was your trip to Spain?

PETER: It was wonderful.

JOHNNIE: Were the people friendly?

PETER: Yes, they were very friendly.

JOHNNIE: What was the weather like?

PETER: It wasn't very good. There was a lot of rain.

JOHNNIE: What were the hotels like?

PETER: Very nice. Everything was good except the weather.

PAIR WORK • *Have conversations like the one on page 71. Use these adjectives to describe the weather and the hotels:* **good, very nice, wonderful, fantastic, bad, not very nice, awful, terrible.**

A: Welcome back, _____. How was

your trip to _____?

B: It was _____.

A: Were the people friendly?

B: _____.

A: What was the weather like?

B: _____.

A: What were the hotels like?

B: _____.

CONVERSATIONS

Listen and read.

PAIR WORK • *Have similar conversations. Answer the questions in the negative.*

1. Where were your friends last weekend? (at home)
2. Where was Maria yesterday? (at the hospital)
3. Where was she last night? (at her apartment)
4. Where were Anne and Barbara last Monday? (at the office)
5. Where was Nick yesterday? (at the garage)
6. Where were the children yesterday afternoon? (at school)
7. Where was Mr. Bascomb last Wednesday? (at the bank)
8. Where were Barbara and Tino last Sunday? (at the park)
9. Where was Tino yesterday? (at the restaurant)

Listen and practice.

BARBARA: Where were you yesterday?

TINO: I was at the beach.

BARBARA: Were you with anyone?

TINO: Yes, I was with a friend named Gina.

BARBARA: Was she young and beautiful?

TINO: No, she wasn't. She was old and ugly.

BARBARA: Are you telling me the truth, Tino?

TINO: Yes, of course.

PAIR WORK • *Ask and answer questions using* ***was*** *and* ***were***. *Use past time expressions such as* ***yesterday, last night, this morning,*** *and so on.*

> alone
> A: **Were you alone last night?**
> B: **Yes, I was.** OR **No, I wasn't. I was with some friends.**

1. at home
2. at the park
3. tired
4. hungry
5. at the library
6. at the post office
7. in a hurry
8. worried
9. sick
10. angry
11. busy
12. free

I was sick.

Listen and repeat.

Nancy likes to fly her airplane.

Otis and Gloria like to walk in the park.

Sam and Mabel want to live on a farm.

Peter wants to visit Africa.

PRACTICE • *Make a sentence about each picture using **like to**.*

1. **Sam and Jimmy like to fish.**

2. **Mabel likes to cook.**

3. Peter _____.

4. Barbara and Tino _____.

5. Dr. Pasto _____.

6. Otis _____.

7. Mr. and Mrs. Bascomb _____.

8. Anne _____.

• *Ask and answer questions about the pictures.*

1. A: **Does Barney like to shave?**
   B: **No, he doesn't.**
   A: **Why not?**
   B: **Because it hurts.**

2. A: **Do Otis and Gloria like to dance?**
   B: **Yes, they do.**
   A: **Why?**
   B: **Because it's fun.**

3. Does Anne like to talk with Dr. Pasto?

4. Does Johnnie like to ride the bus?

5. Do people like to eat at Joe's?

6. Do people like to eat at Mom's?

7. Does Otis like to paint flowers?

8. Do these men like to work?

• *Make a sentence for each picture using **want to**.*

1. Barney
Barney wants to meet Ula Hackey.

2. Sam and Mabel
Sam and Mabel want to rest.

3. Anne

4. Nick

5. Tino and Barbara

6. Mr. Bascomb

7. Jack

8. Gloria and Otis

1. A: **Do Mark and Diane want to get married?**
   B: **Yes, they do.**
   A: **Why?**
   B: **Because they're in love.**

2. A: **Does Albert want to play football?**
   B: **No, he doesn't.**
   A: **Why not?**
   B: **Because he's tired.**

3. Does Bob want to dance with Linda?

4. Does Linda want to ride on Bob's motorcycle?

5. Do the Golos want to eat at Maxim's?

6. Do Mr. and Mrs. Bascomb want to visit Canada?

7. Does Nick want to take a shower?

8. Do the Browns want to buy a clock?

It's Tuesday morning, June 25. Mr. Bascomb is at the bank. He's talking with some businessmen from Chicago. They're representatives of a large toy company. They want to build a toy factory in Wickam City. Mr. Bascomb thinks it's a good idea. He would like to have more new businesses in his city.

"It's good for the economy," says Mr. Bascomb. "New businesses provide more jobs for the people and money for the city."

Mr. Bascomb works long hours and seldom takes a vacation. It's very unusual when he doesn't come to work. Yesterday was an unusual day. Mr. Bascomb wasn't at work. He was at home. He was sick in bed all day. But he wasn't alone. His wife and his dog were there with him.

STORY QUESTIONS

1. What day is it?
2. Where is Mr. Bascomb?
3. Who is he talking to?
4. What do they want to do?
5. Does Mr. Bascomb think it's a good idea? Why?
6. How often does Mr. Bascomb take a vacation?
7. Was he at work yesterday? Why not?
8. Was he alone?

FREE RESPONSE 1 • *Read the story and discuss the questions.*

Mr. Bascomb is a very successful man. He is president of a large bank, and he makes a lot of money. Mr. Bascomb is also a "workaholic." He thinks about his work all the time—it's the most important thing in his life.

1. Do you think Mr. Bascomb has a good life? Why or why not?
2. Do you know people like Mr. Bascomb? What do they do?
3. Do you think people have to be workaholics to be successful?

NEW VOCABULARY • HOUSEWORK

Look at the pictures. What chore is each person doing?

1. Sam is mopping the floor.

2. Mabel is ironing clothes.

3. Linda is vacuuming the living room.

4. Jimmy is taking out the trash.

FREE RESPONSE 2

1. How do you feel about housework?
2. What chores do you like to do?
3. What chores do you hate to do?
4. Who does the cooking in your home?
5. Who washes the dishes?
6. Who does most of the housework?

PAIR WORK • *Ask and answer questions about the pictures on page 81. Use past time expressions such as **yesterday, yesterday afternoon, last night, this morning, last Sunday.***

1. Barbara and Tino/musicians

A: **Where were Barbara and Tino last night?**
B: **They were at a jazz concert.**

A: **What were the musicians like?**
B: **They were excellent (wonderful, marvelous).**

2. Gloria/coffee

A: **Where was Gloria this morning?**
B: **She was at Joe's Coffee Shop.**

A: **What was the coffee like?**
B: **It was terrible (very bad, awful).**

1. Barbara and Tino/musicians

2. Gloria/coffee

3. Peter and Sandy/ weather

4. Anne/weather

5. Albert/pastries

6. Mr. and Mrs. Golo/movie

7. Jimmy and Linda/water

8. Mr. Bascomb/models

Listen and practice.

New York · 68°/43°

A: How was the weather in New York yesterday?

B: It was rainy.

A: What was the high temperature?

B: Sixty-eight degrees.

PAIR WORK • *Have similar conversations about the weather in different cities. Use these adjectives to describe the weather:* **sunny, cloudy, rainy, snowy, windy.**

1. Rio de Janeiro · 90°/72°

2. London · 65°/46°

3. Moscow · 31°/14°

4. Paris · 69°/50°

5. Tokyo · 73°/52°

6. Jerusalem · 87°/62°

PRACTICE • *Answer the questions about the picture.*

1. How many people do you see? What are they doing?
2. How do you think these people are feeling? Why?
3. Do they live on a busy street? Are there many cars?
4. What are the houses like? Are they old or new? Big or small?
5. How is the weather? What time of year do you think it is?
6. What more can you say about this picture?
7. Would you like to live on a street like this? Why or why not?

GROUP WORK • *Talk about the street where you live. Take turns asking questions.*

1. What are the houses like on your street?
2. Are there many trees on your street? What about dogs and cats?
3. What kind of people live on your street? Are there many families with children?
4. Do you know your neighbors? What are they like?
5. Is your street safe or dangerous at night?
6. What kind of transportation do people use where you live? Do most people drive cars, take the bus, or ride bicycles?
7. What is unusual or different about your street? In other words, what makes your street special?
8. Do you like your street? Why or why not?

COMPOSITION • *Write about the street where you live.*

GRAMMAR SUMMARY

Past of TO BE Affirmative

He She I	was	
You We They	were	in Paris yesterday.

Negative

He She I	wasn't (was not)	
You We They	weren't (were not)	in Paris yesterday.

Interrogative

Was	he she I	
Were	you we they	in Paris yesterday?

Short Answers

Yes,	he she I	was.		No,	he she I	wasn't.
	you we they	were.			you we they	weren't.

LIKE TO/WANT TO Affirmative

He She	likes to wants to	get up early. make breakfast. go to the market.
I You We They	like to want to	

Negative

He She	doesn't (does not)	like to want to	get up early. make breakfast. go to the market.
I You We They	don't (do not)		

Interrogative

Does	he she	like to want to	get up early? make breakfast? go to the market?
Do	I you we they		

Short Answers

Yes,	he she	does.		No,	he she	doesn't.
	I you we they	do.			I you we they	don't.

Chapter

6

TOPICS
Leisure activities
Travel
Parties
The beach
Your hometown

GRAMMAR
Simple past: regular and irregular verbs
Wh- questions

FUNCTIONS

Talking about past actions
Talking about your favorite things
Agreeing/disagreeing

Listen and repeat.

1. Yesterday Otis walked to the park.

2. He watched a basketball game.

3. He played chess.

4. He listened to some musicians.

5. Last night the movie started at seven o'clock.

6. It ended at nine o'clock.

1. Last Sunday Anne sang for Barbara and Tino.

2. Dr. Pasto found an African butterfly.

3. Nancy bought a motorcycle.

4. Linda made a birdhouse.

5. Peter drove to the beach.

6. He took his dog with him.

7. They swam in the ocean.

8. Peter lost his car keys.

SIMPLE PAST TENSE OF REGULAR VERBS

She worked in the garden.

____ washed the car.

____ cleaned the kitchen.

____ prepared dinner.

____ rested after dinner.

PRACTICE 1 • *Complete the sentences using the simple past tense.*

They (walk) to the library yesterday.
They walked to the library yesterday.

1. Dr. Pasto (paint) his garage last Sunday.
2. Otis (help) him.
3. They (talk) about the weather.
4. We (enjoy) our dinner last night.
5. Mabel (prepare) chicken and fried potatoes.
6. I (look) at some magazines after dinner.
7. Sam (watch) television.
8. Maria (show) us some pictures of Paris last week.
9. She (live) in France for a year.
10. She (like) the women's clothes.

SIMPLE PAST TENSE OF IRREGULAR VERBS

He got up at eight o'clock.

___ took a shower.

___ had breakfast.

___ read the newspaper.

___ went to work.

PRACTICE 2 • *Make new sentences.*

Peter went to the beach. (I/to the park)
I went to the park.

1. You got up at nine o'clock. (We/at nine thirty)
2. Linda had a hamburger for lunch. (Jimmy/a hot dog)
3. I lost my notebook. (You/your pen)
4. We saw a movie. (Our friends/a football game)
5. Sam took a shower. (Mabel/a bath)
6. Maria bought a vase. (I/a chair)
7. You went to the park. (We/to the beach)
8. Dr. Pasto found a butterfly. (My neighbors/a cat)
9. Mrs. Golo made a chocolate cake. (I/a sandwich)
10. We read the newspaper. (Jack/a magazine)

1

2

1. *Talk about the pictures.*
2. *Listen to the stories.*
3. *Answer the story questions.*

READING

1 Sam Brown lives in California. Last month he went to New York and visited his brother Bob. They talked about old times and looked at family photographs. Sam stayed in New York for a week. He enjoyed his visit very much.

1. Where does Sam Brown live?
2. Where did he go last month?
3. Who did he visit there?
4. What did they talk about?
5. What did they look at?
6. How long did Sam stay in New York?
7. Did he enjoy his visit?

2 Peter Smith had a good time when he was in Spain. He took his camera with him and got some interesting pictures of Madrid. He thought it was a beautiful city. On his last night there he went to a nice little restaurant called La Cocinita. He had chicken and potatoes for dinner and listened to flamenco music. Before he left Spain, Peter bought some postcards for his friends in Wickam City. Johnnie Wilson met him at the airport when he came home.

1. Did Peter have a good time when he was in Spain?
2. What did he take with him?
3. Did he visit Barcelona or Madrid?
4. Where did he go on his last night there?
5. What did he have for dinner?
6. Did he listen to flamenco music or rock music?
7. What did Peter buy for his friends before he left Spain?
8. Who met him at the airport when he returned to Wickam City?

AFFIRMATIVE

Peter went to a famous restaurant.

You _____ .

They _____ .

We _____ .

She _____ .

I _____ .

PRACTICE • *Complete the sentences using the simple past tense.*

Jimmy and Linda (go) to the art museum.
Jimmy and Linda went to the art museum.

1. They (take) the bus.
2. They (meet) their friends at the museum.
3. They (see) some beautiful paintings.
4. Jimmy (like) the paintings from England.
5. Linda (enjoy) everything.
6. They (stay) at the museum for an hour.
7. They (go) to Mom's Cafe for lunch.
8. Linda (have) a bowl of fruit salad.
9. Jimmy (buy) some candy.

Listen and practice.

JIMMY: Did you have a good time in New York, Dad?

SAM: Yes, I did, Jimmy.

JIMMY: What did you and Uncle Bob do?

SAM: We talked about old times.

JIMMY: Did he show you the city?

SAM: Yes, we visited the Statue of Liberty and the United Nations.

JIMMY: Did you see any movies?

SAM: No, but we saw a very interesting play.

JIMMY: When can we go to New York?

SAM: Next year, Jimmy. You and Linda can go with me.

• *Read the first sentence aloud. Then make a negative sentence for each picture.*

1. **Sam went to New York.
   He didn't go to Chicago.**

2. Linda made a birdhouse.

   _____ a doghouse.

3. Nancy bought a motorcycle.

   _____ a car.

4. Otis watched a basketball game.

   _____ a football game.

5. Dr. Pasto found a butterfly.

   _____ a bird.

6. Anne played the guitar.

   _____ the piano.

7. Peter drove to the beach.

   _____ to the park.

8. He took his dog with him.

   _____ his cat with him.

Listen and practice.

ALBERT: Did you go out Saturday night, Linda?

LINDA: Yes, I went to a party.

ALBERT: What did you do there?

LINDA: We sang and danced all night.

ALBERT: Did they have any food?

LINDA: Yes, they had some delicious pastries.

ALBERT: I'm sorry I missed the party.

INTERROGATIVE	SHORT ANSWER FORM

INTERROGATIVE

Did Linda have a good time?

___ Albert _____?

___ they _____?

___ you _____?

SHORT ANSWER FORM

Yes, she did.   No, she didn't.

___, he _____.   ___, he _____.

___, they ____.   ___, they_____.

___, I _____.   ___, I _____.

PRACTICE • *Answer the questions using the short answer form.*

Did Linda stay home Saturday night?
No, she didn't.

Did she go to a party?
Yes, she did.

1. Did she go with Albert?
2. Did she wear jeans?
3. Did she dance at the party?
4. Did they have pastries?
5. Did Sam go to Texas last month?
6. Did he visit his brother?
7. Did they see the Statue of Liberty?
8. Did they go to a movie?
9. Did Sam stay in New York for a month?
10. Did he enjoy his visit?

PAIR WORK 1 • *Ask and answer questions using past time expressions like **yesterday**, **yesterday afternoon, last night, this morning,** and **last Sunday.***

see a movie
A: **Did you see a movie last week?**
B: **Yes, I did.**   OR   **No, I didn't.**

1. go to the park
2. stay home
3. watch television
4. listen to the radio
5. play basketball
6. do your homework
7. take the bus
8. see your friends
9. buy some fruit
10. wash the dishes
11. read the newspaper
12. get a letter

PAIR WORK 2 • *Ask and answer questions as in the conversation below.*

A: Did you have a good time Saturday night/yesterday/last weekend, _____ ?

B: Yes, I did.   OR   No, I didn't.

A: Where did you go?

B: _____.

A: What did you do (there)?

B: _____.

Last Sunday Albert and Jimmy went to the beach. There were hundreds of people there. Jimmy played volleyball and swam in the ocean. But Albert just sat on the beach and watched the girls. It was a hot day and Albert was very thirsty. He wanted a cold drink. Unfortunately, the only restaurant at the beach was closed. The temperature was 90 degrees and Albert was very uncomfortable. Finally he saw a girl with a large picnic basket. It was Jane Garner, a friend from college. Albert carried the basket for her, and she gave him a drink. Five minutes later, Jimmy came and sat with them. They ate and drank and had a good time.

STORY QUESTIONS

1. Where did Albert and Jimmy go last Sunday?
2. How many people were there?
3. What did Jimmy do?
4. What did Albert do?
5. What was the weather like?
6. What did Albert want?
7. Were there any restaurants open?
8. Who did Albert see on the beach?
9. How did he help her?
10. Why did she give Albert a drink?
11. What happened five minutes later?

PRACTICE 1 • *Make questions with **who, what,** or **where.***

> Albert went to the beach.
> **Where did he go?**
>
> He saw Jane Garner.
> **Who did he see?**
>
> She gave him a drink.
> **What did she give him?**

1. Barney went to the market yesterday.
2. He bought some apples and pears.
3. He met Nancy at one o'clock.
4. He gave her an apple.
5. They went to Mom's Cafe for lunch.
6. They sat at the counter.
7. They ordered fried chicken.
8. They saw Tino.
9. He talked about Barbara.
10. She made a cake yesterday.
11. She put the cake on the table.
12. Barbara and Tino ate the cake.

PRACTICE 2 • *Answer the questions.*

> What did Tino bring Barbara? (some flowers)
> **He brought her some flowers.**
>
> What did Jane give Albert? (a drink)
> **She gave him a drink.**

1. What did Peter buy Maria? (some chocolates)
2. What did she bring her friends? (a box of apples)
3. What did they give Barney? (a radio)
4. What did the students bring Mrs. Golo? (a cat)
5. What did she give the cat? (some milk)
6. What did Jack take the Browns? (some old magazines)
7. What did they give Jack? (an old lamp)
8. What did Otis show his friends? (a painting)
9. What did he bring Gloria? (some roses)

PAIR WORK • *Ask and answer questions.*

> corn
> A: **Is corn your favorite vegetable?**
> B: **Yes, it is.** OR **No. Peas are my favorite (vegetable).**

1. red
2. apples
3. coffee
4. ice cream
5. January
6. English
7. football
8. dogs
9. summer
10. roses

corn

peas

PRACTICE • *Change the sentences to the simple past tense.*

1. Mr. Jones lives in San Francisco.
2. He works at the post office.
3. Every morning he gets up at 7:30 and takes a shower.
4. He usually has coffee and eggs for breakfast.
5. Mr. Jones always goes to work at 8:30.
6. He takes the bus to work.
7. He seldom meets people on the bus.
8. Mr. Jones is a quiet man.
9. He doesn't often talk to strangers.

WRITTEN EXERCISE • *Complete the sentences using **because**.*

Barbara takes the bus to work *because she doesn't have a car* .

1. Tino isn't working today _____.
2. Anne is taking her umbrella_____.
3. Peter is wearing a warm coat _____.
4. Mom's Cafe has a lot of customers _____.
5. I'm happy_____.
6. I like my job_____.
7. The teacher is unhappy _____.
8. Linda isn't eating her dinner _____.
9. Sam is resting _____.

FREE RESPONSE • *Do you agree with the statements below? Why?*

"We need more police officers!"
"I agree. We have to stop the criminals."
"I disagree. We already have a lot of police."

1. "Americans are very friendly."
2. "You need friends more than money."
3. "Most people like their jobs."
4. "Candy is good for you."
5. "English is easy."
6. "Most TV programs are boring."
7. "Homework is fun."
8. "Public transportation is terrible."
9. "Most teenagers are good drivers."

PAIR WORK

1. *Ask and answer questions about the pictures.*

> 1: Johnnie
> A: **Where was Johnnie yesterday?**
> B: **He was at home.**
>
> 2: Anne and Nancy
> A: **Where were Anne and Nancy?**
> B: **They were at the park.**

3. Mrs. Golo
4. Sam
5. Peter and Maria
6. Mr. Bascomb
7. Nick
8. Barbara and Tino

2. *Ask and answer questions about the pictures.*

> 1. Johnnie/home
> A: **Was Johnnie at home yesterday?**
> B: **Yes, he was.**
>
> 2. Anne and Nancy/beach
> A: **Were Anne and Nancy at the beach?**
> B: **No, they weren't. They were at the park.**

3. Mrs. Golo/library
4. Sam/garage
5. Peter and Maria/museum
6. Mr. Bascomb/Antique Shop
7. Nick/post office
8. Barbara and Tino/beach

3. *Ask and answer questions about the pictures.*

> 1: Johnnie
> A: **What did Johnnie do yesterday?**
> B: **He painted his house.**
>
> 2: Anne and Nancy
> A: **What did Anne and Nancy do?**
> B: **They played chess.**

3. Mrs. Golo
4. Sam
5. Peter and Maria
6. Mr. Bascomb
7. Nick
8. Barbara and Tino

4. *Ask and answer questions about the pictures.*

> 1. Johnnie/go to the movies
> A: **Did Johnnie go to the movies yesterday?**
> B: **No, he didn't. He painted the house.**
>
> 2. Anne and Nancy/play chess
> A: **Did Anne and Nancy play chess?**
> B: **Yes, they did.**

3. Mrs. Golo/read a book
4. Sam/watch television
5. Peter and Maria/go to the opera
6. Mr. Bascomb/buy a lamp
7. Nick/repair a motorcycle
8. Barbara and Tino/play tennis

FREE RESPONSE • *Answer the questions about yesterday.*

1. Where did you go?
2. Who were you with?
3. What did you do?
4. Did you buy anything?
5. Did you have a good time?
6. How did you go home?
7. What did you have for dinner?
8. What time did you go to bed?
9. What was the last thing you did before you went to bed?

GROUP WORK • *Talk about last weekend. Ask these questions and others of your own.*

1. How was your weekend?
2. Where did you go?
3. Who were you with?
4. What did you do?
5. What happened after that?
6. Did you have a good time?

COMPOSITION • *Write about yesterday, about last weekend, or about any interesting day in the last month. What happened? Did you have fun like Albert and Jimmy did? (See the story on page 95.)*

Listen and practice.

GROUP WORK • *Talk about your hometown. What are the good things about it? What are the bad things? How is it different from the city you're living in now?*

GRAMMAR SUMMARY

SIMPLE PAST Affirmative		
He She I You We They	walked drove took the bus	to class last week.

Negative			
He She I You We They	didn't (did not)	walk drive take the bus	last week.

Interrogative			
Did	he she I you we they	walk drive take the bus	last week?

Short Answers					
Yes,	he she I you we they	did.	No,	he she I you we they	didn't.

SIMPLE PAST Irregular Verbs		
He	bought ate took found had	some candy yesterday.

Regular Verbs		
They	danced talked	at the party.
	worked lived	in New York.

Questions with WHERE, WHEN, WHO, WHAT	
Where did Anne go?	To the park.
When did she leave?	12 o'clock.
Who did she meet?	Nancy.
What did they play?	Chess.

Chapter 7

TOPICS
Plans for the near future
Movies

GRAMMAR
Future with "going to"
Adverbs of manner

FUNCTIONS
Expressing intention
Describing how people do things
Asking for and giving information
Giving opinions

1

2

3

4

1. *Talk about the pictures.*
2. *Listen to the stories.*
3. *Answer the story questions.*

READING

1 Peter is packing his suitcase. He's preparing for another trip. Tomorrow he's going to travel to France. He's going to stay in Paris for a week. He's going to visit the Eiffel Tower.

1. What's Peter doing?
2. What's he going to do tomorrow?
3. How long is he going to stay in Paris?
4. What's he going to do there?

2 Albert is picking up the phone. He's going to call Linda. He's going to invite her to a movie. He's going to drive his father's car.

1. What's Albert doing?
2. Who's he going to call?
3. Is he going to invite her to a movie or a concert?
4. Is he going to take a taxi or drive his father's car?

3 Mrs. Brown went to the market this morning. She bought some chocolate, eggs, flour, and sugar. She's going to make a chocolate cake for Jimmy. It's his birthday tomorrow. He's going to have a party.

1. Where did Mrs. Brown go this morning?
2. What did she buy?
3. What's she going to make?
4. When's Jimmy going to have his party?

4 Tino is at the flower shop. He's looking at some flowers. He's going to buy some carnations. He's going to give them to Barbara.

1. Where's Tino?
2. What's he looking at?
3. What's he going to buy?
4. Who's he going to give them to?

FUTURE WITH "GOING TO": AFFIRMATIVE

Peter's going to stay in Paris.	We're going to visit London.
He's _____.	They're _____.
Mary's _____.	You're _____.
She's _____.	I'm _____.

PRACTICE • *Answer the questions about the stories.*

> Is Peter going to travel <u>to England</u>?
> **No, he's going to travel to France.**

1. Is he going to stay in Paris <u>for a month</u>?
2. Is he going to visit <u>the Tower of London</u>?
3. Is Albert going to call <u>Jane</u>?
4. Is he going to invite her <u>to a concert</u>?
5. Is he going to drive <u>his mother's car</u>?
6. Is Mrs. Brown going to make <u>an orange cake</u>?
7. Is Jimmy going to have his birthday party <u>next week</u>?
8. Is Tino going to buy <u>some roses</u>?
9. Is he going to give them <u>to Maria</u>?

Listen and practice.

MABEL BROWN: What are you going to do this weekend?

SAM BROWN: I'm going to plant some banana trees.

MABEL BROWN: Where are you going to plant them?

SAM BROWN: In back of the house.

MABEL BROWN: What are you going to do then?

SAM BROWN: I'm going to sit down and relax.

JIMMY: What are you going to do tonight?

LINDA: I'm going to see a movie with Albert.

JIMMY: With Albert? But he doesn't have a car.

LINDA: He's going to drive his father's car.

PRACTICE • *Read the first sentence. Then make a negative sentence for each picture.*

1. Sam is going to plant banana trees.
   He isn't going to plant apple trees.

2. Linda and Albert are going to see a movie.
   They aren't going to see a play.

3. Dr. Pasto is going to play the piano.
   _____ the violin.

4. Otis and Gloria are going to eat at Mom's.
   _____ at Joe's.

5. The Farleys are going to take the bus.
   _____ a taxi.

6. Suzi is going to wear her red dress.
   _____ her green dress.

7. Robert is going to call his girlfriend.
   _____ his sister.

8. Barbara and Tino are going to play tennis.
   _____ baseball.

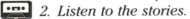

1. *Talk about the pictures.*
2. *Listen to the stories.*
3. *Answer the story questions.*

1 Barbara is a good secretary. She types quickly and accurately. She listens carefully and doesn't make mistakes. Barbara works very well.

1. What kind of secretary is Barbara?
2. How does she type?
3. Does she listen carefully?
4. Does she make mistakes?
5. How does she work?

2 Anne is a bad secretary. She types slowly and makes a lot of mistakes. She doesn't listen carefully and works badly.

1. What kind of secretary is Anne?
2. How does she type?
3. Does she make mistakes?
4. Does she listen carefully?
5. How does she work?

ADJECTIVES
She's a good typist.
_____ bad _____.
_____ slow _____.
_____ quick _____.
_____ careful _____.

ADVERBS OF MANNER
She types well.
_____ badly.
_____ slowly.
_____ quickly.
_____ carefully.

WRITTEN EXERCISE • *Change the sentences using adverbs.*

Anne is a slow worker. *She works slowly.*

Dr. Pasto is a good speaker. *He speaks well.*

1. Jack is a good cook._____

2. He's a dangerous driver. _____

3. Fred is a careful writer. _____

4. He's a slow reader._____

5. Mrs. Golo is a bad dancer. _____

6. She's a good singer. _____

7. Barbara is a quick typist. _____

8. She's a careful driver._____

CONVERSATION

 Listen and practice.

MR. BASCOMB: You're working slowly, Miss Jones.

ANNE JONES: That's because I'm working carefully.

MR. BASCOMB: But you make a lot of mistakes.

ANNE JONES: I know, Mr. Bascomb.

MR. BASCOMB: Perhaps I don't speak clearly.

ANNE JONES: No, I understand you perfectly.

MR. BASCOMB: Then what's the problem?

ANNE JONES: I don't know, Mr. Bascomb.

1. Mrs. Golo

2. Barbara

3. Jack

4. Barney

5. Otis and Gloria

6. Anne

7. Albert

8. Fred

WRITTEN EXERCISE • *Write a sentence about each picture using an adverb.*

1. (loud) Mrs. Golo *speaks loudly* _____ .

2. (soft) Barbara_____ .

3. (dangerous) Jack_____ .

4. (careful) Barney_____ .

5. (good) Otis and Gloria _____ .

6. (beautiful) Anne _____ .

7. (quick) Albert_____ .

8. (slow) Fred _____ .

PAIR WORK • *Ask and answer questions about the pictures.*

1. A: **Does Mrs. Golo speak loudly?**
   B: **Yes, she does.**
2. A: **Does Barbara speak loudly?**
   B: **No, she doesn't.**

3. Does Jack drive carefully?
4. Does Barney drive carefully?
5. Do Otis and Gloria dance badly?
6. Does Anne sing beautifully?
7. Does Albert eat quickly?
8. Does Fred read quickly?

FREE RESPONSE • *Describe how you do each activity. Use the adverbs* **quickly, slowly, carefully, well, badly, loudly, softly** *and* **beautifully.**

sing
I sing well.

walk
I walk quickly.

1. dance
2. play chess
3. read
4. walk
5. eat
6. write
7. speak
8. dress
9. work
10. sing

There's a big crowd of people at the Odeon Theater tonight.
They're waiting anxiously for Ula Häckey, the famous Hollywood
actress. She's going to attend the premiere of her new film, *Sweet
Summer.* Everyone is very excited. Miss Hackey is coming now.
She's waving happily to the crowd. The man next to her is a
television announcer. He's going to ask Miss Hackey some
questions about her new film. There are some photographers
following the actress. They're going to take pictures of her for the
newspapers. She's a very popular star. After the film, Miss Hackey
is going to sign autographs and talk to the people.

STORY QUESTIONS

1. Who are the people waiting for?
2. Why is she at the Odeon Theater tonight?
3. Who is the man next to Miss Hackey?
4. What's he going to do?
5. Who are the men following the actress?
6. What are they going to do?
7. What is Miss Hackey going to do after the film?
8. Why do you think Miss Hackey is so popular?
9. Who is your favorite movie star?

FREE RESPONSE

1. What are you going to do after class?
2. Are you going to walk home?
3. What are you going to do when you get home?
4. What are you going to have for dinner?
5. What are you going to do tonight?
6. What time are you going to get up in the morning?
7. What are you going to do tomorrow?
8. Are you going to see your friends tomorrow?
9. What are you going to do this weekend?

WRITTEN EXERCISE • *Complete the sentences using suitable adjectives. There can be more than one suitable adjective for each sentence.*

I don't like this chair. It's *ugly (too big) (uncomfortable)* .

1. Put on your coat. It's _____ outside.

2. Gloria is _____ because she can't find her keys.

3. You need an umbrella on _____ days.

4. There's nobody with that woman. She's _____.

5. Is there any food in the refrigerator? I'm _____.

6. You're going to like this cake. It's _____.

7. Please wash the dishes. They're _____.

8. Joe is a _____ man. He's married to a beautiful woman.

9. She loves coffee. It's her _____ drink.

10. She puts ketchup in her coffee. Isn't that _____?

11. Marty never comes on time. He's always _____.

12. We all make mistakes. Nobody's _____.

1. Peter

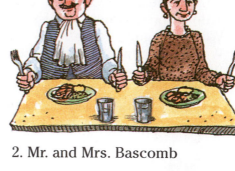

2. Mr. and Mrs. Bascomb

3. Jack

4. Anne

5. Jimmy and his friends

6. Barney

7. Tino

8. Gloria and Otis

PAIR WORK I • *Ask and answer questions about the pictures.*

> 1. Peter
> A: **What's Peter going to do?**
> B: **He's going to wash the car.**
>
> 2. Mr. and Mrs. Bascomb
> A: **What are Mr. and Mrs. Bascomb going to do?**
> B: **They are going to eat dinner.**

3. Jack 6. Barney
4. Anne 7. Tino
5. Jimmy and his friends 8. Otis and Gloria

PAIR WORK 2 • *Ask and answer questions about the pictures.*

> 1. Peter/wash the dishes?
> A: **Is Peter going to wash the dishes?**
> B: **No, he isn't. He's going to wash the car.**
>
> 2. Mr. and Mrs. Bascomb/eat dinner?
> A: **Are Mr. and Mrs. Bascomb going to eat dinner?**
> B: **Yes, they are.**

3. Jack/shave 6. Barney/take a bath
4. Anne/call the fire department 7. Tino/buy some candy
5. Jimmy and his friends/play tennis 8. Otis and Gloria/play chess

WRITTEN EXERCISE • *Complete the sentences using these adverbs: **happily, well, badly, quickly, carefully, softly, immediately, warmly, slowly, loudly, easily**. Use each adverb only once.*

> Jimmy ate _*quickly*_ because he was in a hurry.

1. People usually speak _____ in the library.

2. Mr. Bascomb walked _____ up the stairs. He was very tired.

3. He can't see very _____ without his glasses.

4. Ula Hackey has a big car. It can _____ hold five passengers.

5. We always dress _____ on cold days.

6. Anne really needs dancing lessons. She dances very _____.

7. The people next door talk very _____. You can hear them through the walls.

8. The children are playing _____ in the front yard. They're all laughing.

9. I need you right away. Please come _____.

10. The streets are dangerous. Drive _____.

PAIR WORK • *Look at the movie poster and complete the dialogue.*

OTIS: Hi, Gloria.

GLORIA: Hello, Otis.

OTIS: What are you going to do tonight?

GLORIA: I'm going _____.

OTIS: Oh, really? What's the name of the movie?

GLORIA: It's called _____.

OTIS: Is it a comedy?

GLORIA: No. _____.

OTIS: Who's in it?

GLORIA: _____.

OTIS: Is she a good actress?

GLORIA: Yes. _____.

OTIS: Where's the movie playing?

GLORIA: _____.

OTIS: Is that on Maple Street?

GLORIA: No. _____.

OTIS: What time does the first show start?

GLORIA: _____. Why don't you come?

OTIS: Sure, why not? I like love stories, too.

GROUP WORK • *Talk about movies. Ask these questions and others of your own.*

1. What kind of movies do you like—comedies, love stories, action-adventure?
2. Do you have favorite actors? actresses? Why do you like them?
3. What's your favorite movie? Who's in it? What's the story about?

GRAMMAR SUMMARY

GOING TO   Affirmative

He She	's (is)		see a movie.
I	'm (am)	going to	play tennis.
You We They	're (are)		visit Paris.

Negative

He She	isn't 's not (is not)		see a movie.
I	'm not (am not)	going to	play tennis.
You We They	aren't 're not (are not)		visit Paris.

Interrogative

Is	he she		see a movie?
Am	I	going to	play tennis?
Are	you we they		visit Paris?

Short Answers

Yes,	he she	is.	No,	he she	isn't.
	I	am.		I	'm not.
	you we they	are.		you we they	aren't.

Questions with WHERE, WHEN, WHO, WHAT

Where's he going to work?	In London.
When's he going to leave?	Next month.
Who's he going to write to?	His wife.
What's he going to buy?	A suitcase.

Questions with HOW

How does she	work? drive?

ADVERBS OF MANNER

She	works drives	well. badly. slowly. quickly. carefully.

Review Chapter

TOPICS

Travel
Department stores
Physical problems
Medical appointments

Job safety
Telephone communication
Leisure activities

GRAMMAR

Review

FUNCTIONS

Asking about and indicating location
Talking about daily activities in the present and past
Expressing intention
Describing physical problems
Making appointments
Writing telephone messages

Last summer Nancy Paine flew around the world. She started in New York and made her first stop in Rio de Janeiro. Rio is a wonderful city and Nancy made some good friends there. They taught her a few words of Portuguese and she learned the samba.

After a week in Rio, Nancy continued her journey. She flew over some very high mountains called the Andes and landed in Lima, Peru. She walked around the capital and took photographs of the beautiful old churches. Nancy left Peru on a fine, sunny day. She traveled across the Pacific Ocean to the island of Tahiti.

It was a very long trip, more than two thousand miles. But the weather was good, and she didn't have any problems. Nancy loved the people of Tahiti, and she had a good time there. She sailed a small boat and swam in the ocean every day. The sun was always hot and the beaches were beautiful. Everything was perfect.

After two weeks Nancy got back in her plane and left for Japan. She stayed in Tokyo for a couple of days, in a small hotel near the center of the city. She found a very nice teahouse across the street from her hotel. Nancy enjoyed the lovely gardens there. She also admired the traditional clothes of the Japanese women.

Nancy's next stop was Moscow, Russia. She had some rough weather on the way. But Nancy is an expert pilot, and she arrived at her destination without any serious trouble. In Moscow she bought a fur coat and saw some folk dancers.

The last stop on Nancy's journey was Paris, the "City of Light." She visited some friends in the Latin Quarter, and they took her to a fine restaurant near the river Seine. Nancy ate frog legs and drank some delicious white wine. Her friends asked a lot of questions about her travels, and she told them everything. It was quite a journey.

STORY QUESTIONS

1. What did Nancy do last summer?
2. Where did she make her first stop?
3. What did Nancy learn in Rio?
4. Where did she go after Brazil?
5. What did she do in Lima?
6. Did Nancy have a good time in Tahiti? What did she do there?
7. How long did Nancy stay in Tokyo?
8. What did she admire about the Japanese women?
9. What was Nancy's next stop? What did she do there?
10. Who did Nancy visit when she was in Paris?
11. Where did they take her?
12. What did they talk about?

FREE RESPONSE

1. When was the last time you took a trip?
2. Where did you go? Who did you go with?
3. Did you have a good time? What did you do?
4. Did you meet any interesting people?
5. What was the best part of your trip?

WRITTEN EXERCISE • *Read the sentences. Then write sentences using* **can't** + *verbs from the list below. Use each verb only once.*

understand	listen to	call	write (to)
drink	wear	buy	drive
read	open	play	sing

I don't have her phone number. *I can't call her.*

This book is boring. *I can't read it.*

1. This shirt is dirty. _____
2. I don't have their address. _____
3. He's talking in Chinese. _____
4. That car isn't mine. _____
5. I don't have the key to the garage. _____
6. The guitar is broken. _____
7. She sings terribly. _____
8. I don't know the words to that song. _____
9. This coffee is cold. _____
10. That camera is too expensive. _____

Listen and practice.

A: Excuse me. Do you sell eye shadow?

B: Yes, it's in the cosmetics department.

A: Where's the cosmetics department?

B: It's on the first floor.

A: Excuse me. Do you sell dressers?

B: Yes, they're in the furniture department.

A: Where's the furniture department?

B: It's on the third floor.

PAIR WORK • *Have similar conversations.*

1. dishes
2. perfume
3. chairs
4. couches
5. lipstick
6. cups
7. cologne
8. tables
9. pans
10. lamps
11. bath soap
12. coffeepots

PRACTICE

1. Look at the pictures of Peter and make sentences about what he is doing now.

> 1. He's getting up.

2. Make sentences about what he does every day.

> 1. He gets up.

3. Make sentences about what he did yesterday.

> 1. He got up.

WRITTEN EXERCISE • *Complete the sentences with an adjective or an adverb.*

> The old man walked __*slowly*__ down the street. (slow/slowly)
>
> He had a __*sad*__ look on his face. (sad/sadly)

1. Gloria smiled_____at her boyfriend. (happy/happily)

2. She has a_____smile. (beautiful/beautifully)

3. I'm not a very_____musician. (good/well)

4. I play the piano_____. (bad/badly)

5. Your bed isn't very_____. (comfortable/comfortably)

6. Do you sleep_____at night? (good/well)

7. It's_____cold today. (terrible/terribly)

8. I'm glad I have a_____jacket. (warm/warmly)

9. Be_____when you cross the street. (careful/carefully)

10. People drive_____around here. (dangerous/dangerously)

FREE RESPONSE

1. How do most people get around in this city? Do they walk, drive, or take the bus?
2. How do you get around? Do you always use the same kind of transportation?
3. Do you know what street the post office is on? the library? the hospital?
4. Do you know a good place to shop for food? What kind of food do you buy?
5. Are you a good cook? What can you make?
6. Do you sleep well at night? How much sleep do you need?
7. How often do you watch television? What programs do you watch?
8. Do you like to play sports? Which ones?
9. Do you like to dance? Where do you go to dance?
10. Where do you go to have fun?

WRITTEN EXERCISE • *Complete the sentences using the simple past tense.*

> Tino___*went*___to the florist and ___*bought*___some flowers. (go/buy)

1. Barney_____all day yesterday. (work)

2. He_____a lot of tourists at the airport. (meet)

3. He_____them to the Wickam Hotel. (take)

4. After work he_____to Nick's Garage. (go)

5. His friends_____all there. (be)

6. They_____sodas and_____cards. (drink/play)

7. Barney_____every game. He never_____. (win/lose)

8. He_____a good time with his friends. (have)

9. Barney_____the garage at eight-thirty. (leave)

10. He_____in his taxi and_____home. (get/drive)

READING: A MYSTERIOUS COUPLE

Daisy Humple has a small apartment near the center of Wickam City. Her boyfriend, Simon, is a magician. He lives a long way from Daisy, on the other side of town. Every weekend he appears at her apartment. He usually brings her chocolates or flowers. He pulls them out of his hat. Sometimes Daisy and Simon play cards. He always wins, and Daisy thinks he is lucky. Actually, Simon never loses at cards or any other game. He is a very clever man. He is also very amusing. He tells a lot of funny stories, and Daisy always laughs. Simon and Daisy are very happy together, but they're a mysterious couple. They often disappear on weekends, and nobody knows where they go.

STORY QUESTIONS

1. Where is Daisy's apartment?
2. What is her boyfriend's name?
3. Does he live near Daisy?
4. When does he come to her apartment?
5. What does he usually bring her?
6. Who always wins when Simon and Daisy play cards?
7. Why does Daisy laugh when she is with Simon?
8. Why are Simon and Daisy a mysterious couple?

WRITTEN EXERCISE • *Change the story about Simon and Daisy to the simple past tense.*

Listen and practice.

PAIR WORK • *Have similar conversations.*

①

②

③

④

⑤

⑥

Listen and practice.

ANNE: What's wrong with Mr. Bascomb? He doesn't look very well.

BARBARA: He has a stomachache. It's really bothering him.

ANNE: That's too bad. I hope he feels better soon.

BARBARA: Me, too.

PAIR WORK • *Have similar conversations about the pictures below.*

A: What's wrong with _____? He/She doesn't look very well.

B: He/She has a _____. It's really bothering him/her.

A: That's too bad. I hope he/she feels better soon.

B: Me, too.

1. Mrs. Golo
   headache

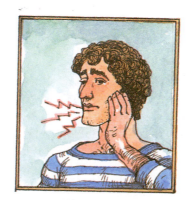

2. Tino
   toothache

3. Suzi Suzuki
   backache

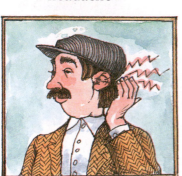

4. Barney
   earache

5. Gloria
   sore throat

6. Peter
   cold

🔊 *Listen and practice.*

MR. BASCOMB: I want to make an appointment with Dr. Feelgood.

RECEPTIONIST: What's your name?

MR. BASCOMB: *John Bascomb.*

RECEPTIONIST: What's the matter?

MR. BASCOMB: I have a *bad stomachache.*

RECEPTIONIST: Can you come in this afternoon?

MR. BASCOMB: No, I have a *business meeting* this afternoon.

RECEPTIONIST: A business meeting?

MR. BASCOMB: Yes, it's very important. I can't miss my meeting.

RECEPTIONIST: Well, when can you come?

MR. BASCOMB: I can come tomorrow.

RECEPTIONIST: OK. The doctor can see you tomorrow at two o'clock.

MR. BASCOMB: That's fine. See you tomorrow.

PAIR WORK • *Have similar conversations. Use the information in the pictures below.*

1. Florence Golo
   bad headache
   dance lesson

2. Tino Martinoli
   toothache
   tennis game

3. Suzi Suzùki
   backache
   cooking class

4. Barney Field
   earache
   piano lesson

5. Gloria Cole
   sore throat
   date with Otis

6. Peter Smith
   bad cold
   business meeting

JOB SAFETY

WRITTEN EXERCISE • *Look at the safety violations.*
Choose a sentence for each picture.

Move those boxes!	Watch out!	No drinking!
Use your rubber gloves!	Turn off the gas!	No talking!
Put on your hard hat!	Don't stand there!	No smoking!

hard hat   rubber gloves

GROUP WORK • *Do you think these jobs are dangerous? What are some other dangerous jobs? List three jobs that you think are dangerous and explain why. For example: A window-washer's job is dangerous because you can fall.*

130   Chapter 8 • Review

CONVERSATION

Listen and practice.

SAM: Hello.

BOB: Hello. Can I speak to Linda, please?

SAM: Linda isn't here. Would you like to leave a message?

BOB: Yes. Please ask her to call Bob. My number is 555–3924.

SAM: OK. I'll give her the message.

BOB: Thanks a lot. Good-bye.

SAM: Good-bye.

·MESSAGE·
Linda
Call Bob
555-3924
Dad

WRITTEN EXERCISE • *Look at the message Sam wrote down for Linda. Then listen to the telephone calls to Gloria and Tino and write down the messages.*

· MESSAGE·
Gloria

· MESSAGE·
Tino

PAIR WORK • *Have similar conversations. Student A calls Student B and leaves a message for a friend.*

FREE RESPONSE

1. How often do you use the phone?
2. How many phones do you have? Where are they?
3. How much is your phone bill?
4. Who do you call? What do you talk about?
5. Do you ever make long distance calls? If so, to where?
6. When the phone rings in your home, who usually answers it?
7. Do you ever get strange or unusual calls?
8. Do you answer the phone when you're busy?
9. Do you have an answering machine?
10. How do you feel when you talk to an answering machine?

Hello, you have two messages.

ON OFF   PLAY MESSAGES

answering machine

A day in the life of Julian Mayberry.

GROUP WORK • *Tell the story of Julian Mayberry. One student describes the first picture, another student describes the second picture, and so on.*

A: Julian is sitting by the phone. He's feeling depressed because no one calls him.

ROLE PLAY • *Make up a conversation between Julian and his new friend, Archie. What do you think they are saying to each other at the bus stop?*

CLASS ACTIVITY • *Are the people at Archie's having a good time? Who is and who isn't?*

1. Julian
2. Lisa
3. Ed
4. Archie
5. Rico
6. Candy
7. Gladys
8. Johnnie

GROUP WORK 1 • *Give your opinion of these people.*

beautiful	*disgusting	intelligent
boring	friendly	*selfish
charming	funny	*shy
dangerous	handsome	stupid

*new vocabulary

1. Julian
A: **I think he's nice.**
B: **I think he's interesting.**
C: **I don't agree. I think he's boring.**

GROUP WORK 2 • *Talk about a party you went to. Did you have a good time? What did you do? Did you meet any interesting people? What were they like?*

Talk about the people in the pictures. What are they going to do this weekend?

1. **Barbara is going to have a date with Tino. She's going to wear her new dress. They're going to have dinner in a fancy restaurant. After dinner they're going to dance at Ciro's. They're going to have a wonderful time.**

2. Sam is going to take his family to the beach . . .

3. Anne is going to sleep until noon . . .

4. Jenny and Marty are going to ride their bicycles to the Rex Theater . . .

PAIR WORK • *Talk about your plans for the weekend. What are you going to do?*

COMPOSITION • *Write about what you're going to do this weekend.*

WRITTEN EXERCISE • *Complete the sentences using suitable nouns. There can be more than one suitable noun for each sentence.*

The bus can hold forty *passengers* .

1. I talked with Alice last night. We had an interesting _____ .

2. She isn't very pretty, but she has a good _____ .

3. Alice is married. Her _____ works at the post office.

4. He works during the day and studies in the _____ .

5. Can you get a good _____ in the public schools?

6. That's a good question, but I don't have the _____ .

7. I like Sam and Mabel. They're nice _____ .

8. They're planting tomatoes in their _____ .

9. Canada is a beautiful _____ , but it gets very cold in

   the _____ .

10. We're going to Mexico on our next _____ .

11. I'm an American. What's your _____ ?

12. I can speak English, Spanish, and French. How many_____
    can you speak?

FREE RESPONSE

1. Are you usually on time?
2. What do you say when you're late?
3. Do you wait for your friends when they're late? How long do you wait?
4. What language do you speak with your friends?
5. How often do you speak English outside of class?
6. Where did you have lunch yesterday? What did you eat?
7. How is the weather today? Is this a good day for a picnic?
8. Are you busy this week? What are some things you have to do?
9. How do you relax? Do you like to read, or listen to music?
10. What is your favorite pastime?

1. Nancy traveled _____ the world.
   - a. over
   - b. on
   - c. across
   - d. around

2. She flew _____ high mountains.
   - a. over
   - b. under
   - c. at
   - d. in

3. She was _____ Paris last month.
   - a. to
   - b. at
   - c. in
   - d. from

4. Jack asked me a lot of questions _____ my job.
   - a. of
   - b. about
   - c. for
   - d. on

5. Where did you go yesterday? I went _____ the library.
   - a. at
   - b. in
   - c. for
   - d. to

6. Is this computer _____ ?
   - a. your
   - b. yours
   - c. to you
   - d. you

7. The boys are washing _____ clothes.
   - a. their
   - b. they're
   - c. there
   - d. theirs

8. Whose car is that?
   - a. her
   - b. to her
   - c. hers
   - d. Mrs. Jacobs

9. I'm taking _____ some chocolates.
   - a. her
   - b. to her
   - c. hers
   - d. she

10. He's telling _____ an amusing story.
    - a. they
    - c them
    - b. to them
    - d. their

11. Don't talk _____ .
    - a. him
    - b. he
    - c. to him
    - d. at him

12. _____ coffee in the pot.
    - a. It's a
    - b. It has
    - c. There's a
    - d. There's some

13. _____ magazines in the closet.
    - a. They're
    - b. Their
    - c. There's a
    - d. There are

14. _____ bottle in the sink.
    - a. It's a
    - b. There's a
    - c. It has a
    - d. There are

15. She _____ the bus every day.
    - a. taking
    - b. is taking
    - c. takes
    - d. take

16. I never _____ coffee.
    - a. drink
    - b. am drinking
    - c. drinks
    - d. to drink

17. He _____ today.
    - a. are working
    - b. is working
    - c. work
    - d. working

18. Look! They _____ in the street.
    - a. is playing
    - b. plays
    - c. play
    - d. are playing

19. Does Anne like music? Yes, she _____ .
    - a. do
    - b. likes
    - c. does
    - d. does like

20. Do they always watch television? Yes, they _____ .
    - a. watch
    - b. do
    - c. do watch
    - d. does

21. I don't need _____ money.
    a. some   c. another
    b. any   d. one

22. We bought _____ food.
    a. some   c. a
    b. any   d. one

23. She doesn't have any sugar
    She needs _____ .
    a. any   c. some
    b. one   d. another

24. They _____ in New York last week.
    a. are   c. was
    b. went   d. were

25. Maria _____ at home yesterday.
    a. is   c. were
    b. was   d. went

26. Did she _____ that movie?
    a. go   c. see
    b. look   d. saw

27. Sam didn't _____ to the meeting.
    a. come   c. comes
    b. came   d. coming

28. He _____ home last night.
    a. stay   c. is staying
    b. stays   d. stayed

29. Did Mabel wash the dishes?
    Yes, she _____ .
    a. did   c. wash
    b. did wash   d. washed

30. Did they have chicken for dinner?
    No, they _____ .
    a. didn't have   c. have not
    b. didn't   d. don't

31. They ate _____ because they were in a hurry.
    a. well   c. quickly
    b. slowly   d. carefully

32. The streets are dangerous.
    Drive _____ .
    a. happily   c. accurately
    b. quickly   d. carefully

33. Gloria is a good dancer.
    She dances _____ .
    a. well   c. goodly
    b. good   d. fine

34. Otis is _____ .
    a. one artist c. an artist
    b. a artist   d. artist

35. Are you a tourist?
    No, I _____ here.
    a. come   c. travel
    b. live   d. visit

36. Mrs. Golo is sick. Call a _____ .
    a. policeman   c. mechanic
    b. repairman   d. doctor

37. I'm going to the market to _____ some milk.
    a. buy   c. drink
    b. borrow   d. have

38. You need an umbrella on _____ days.
    a. windy   c. sunny
    b. rainy   d. cloudy

39. It's always hot _____ the summer
    a. at   c. in
    b. on   d. for

40. How was your vacation?

It was _____ .

a. wonderful   c. in Brazil
b. two weeks   d. $1,000.00

41. Jack is resting _____ he's tired.

a. but   c. and
b. because   d. or

42. I can't sing very well, _____ I can play the guitar.

a. but   c. and
b. because   d. or

43. You're smart. You never make the _____ mistake twice.

a. second   c. same
b. different   d. other

44. Nancy is a pilot.

a. She takes care of sick people.
b. She drives people everywhere.
c. She repairs cars.
d. She flies airplanes.

45. What's your occupation?

a. I'm a teacher.
b. I'm busy.
c. I work here.
d. I have a job.

46. Mr. Moto _____ his motorcycle to work.

a. flies   c. rides
b. drives   d. runs

47. Linda has a lot of friends.

She's very _____ .

a. popular   c. funny
b. famous   d. lonely

48. We're waiting for Marty.

He's _____ again.

a. early   c. late
b. on time   d. ready

49. _____ Can I talk with you for a minute?

a. No problem.
b. Excuse me.
c. Be careful.
d. You're welcome.

50. What's wrong?

a. You're right.
b. Of course.
c. That's too bad.
d. I don't feel well.

G R A M M A R
Must
Future with "will"
Would
Should

STRUCTURE • MUST

We use **must** to express necessity.

WRITTEN EXERCISE • *Write a sentence for each picture. Start with "You must . . ."*

see a doctor	stop smoking	call me
wear a coat and tie	eat your spinach	be quiet
do your homework	be home by midnight	visit us again sometime

PAIR WORK • *Talk about the pictures. What's happening?*

We use **will** when we decide to do something at the time of speaking.

WRITTEN EXERCISE • Complete the sentences with **I'll** (I will) + verb: **show, get, answer, eat, make, go.**

PAIR WORK • Practice these conversations with a partner.

We often use **would** to make requests. With **please** the sentence is more polite.

WRITTEN EXERCISES • *Write a request for each picture. Start with "Would you . . .?"*

iron my shirt	be quiet	take out the trash
mail these letters	answer the phone	pass me the ketchup
turn off the radio	give this package to Mr. Bascomb	open the window

PAIR WORK • *Make two requests of your partner.*

GROUP WORK • *Talk about the pictures. What's happening?*

*We often use **should** when we give advice.*

WRITTEN EXERCISE • *Write a sentence for each picture. Start with "You should . . ."*

do your homework	use your knife and fork	take a bath
get a haircut	ask Alice to dance	get some rest
take some aspirin	go to the dentist	brush your teeth after every meal

PAIR WORK • *List three things each of you should do.*

Appendix

Infinitive	Past Tense	Infinitive	Past Tense
be	was/were	make	made
bring	brought	meet	met
buy	bought	put	put
come	came	read	read
cut	cut	ride	rode
do	did	see	saw
drink	drank	shine	shone
drive	drove	sing	sang
eat	ate	sit	sat
feed	fed	speak	spoke
find	found	stand	stood
fly	flew	swim	swam
forget	forgot	take	took
get	got	teach	taught
give	gave	tell	told
go	went	think	thought
have	had	understand	understood
hold	held	wear	wore
know	knew	win	won
leave	left	write	wrote
lose	lost		

TAPESCRIPT FOR PAGE 131

LISA: Hello.

OTIS: Hi, Lisa. It's Otis.

LISA: Hi, Otis.

OTIS: Is Gloria there?

LISA: No, she went out. Do you want to leave a message?

OTIS: Yes. Tell her the jazz concert is at 9 o'clock.

LISA: OK. I'll give her the message.

OTIS: Thanks, Lisa. Good-bye.

LISA: Bye bye.

MR. MARTINOLI: Martinoli Restaurant. May I help you?

BARBARA: Hi, Mr. Martinoli. It's Barbara.

MR. MARTINOLI: Hello, Barbara. Tino's not here now. Can I take a message?

BARBARA: Yes, please. Tell Tino to meet me at the bank after work.

MR. MARTINOLI: OK. I'll tell him.

BARBARA: Thanks a lot. Bye bye.

MR. MARTINOLI: Good-bye.

CHAPTER ONE

s

eats	helps	wants
drinks	works	makes
smokes	paints	walks

Otis never smokes or drinks.

He often walks to the park
and paints pictures.

z

plays	drives	calls
wears	cleans	gives
lives	reads	shows

Mrs. Bascomb seldom calls her friends.

She lives in a beautiful house and drives
a big car.

iz

watches	washes	crosses
dances	brushes	kisses
	closes	

Barbara always brushes her hair and washes her face.

She sometimes watches television.

CHAPTER TWO

o

only	coat	those
open	cold	show
rose	phone	window
home	know	

Don't open those envelopes.

The yellow roses are by the window.

a

clock	stop	coffee
often	pot	doctor
hot	shop	across
dog	closet	modern

Tom often stops at the coffee shop.

He eats a lot of hot dogs.

CHAPTER THREE

eyr

hair	pear	very
wear	chair	airport
care	where	repair
there	their	dictionary

Where's their dictionary?

There's a pear on the chair.

er

her	dirty	work
skirt	modern	dinner
under	word	after
counter	dancer	learn

Her hamburger is on the counter.

The singer and dancer want dessert after dinner.

CHAPTER FIVE

a

sock	often	economy
shop	pocket	politics
job	across	doctor
box	bottle	coffee

The doctor often walks to his office.

Tom wants some hot coffee.

ae

can	sandwich	bank
hat	dancer	stamp
black	glass	plant
apple	Spanish	shampoo

Sam can understand Spanish.

Nancy is asking for a glass of apple juice.

CHAPTER SIX

id

painted	needed	waited
rested	repeated	started
wanted	visited	ended

He painted the house and visited his sister.

The movie started at seven and ended at nine.

She repeated the question and waited for an answer.

d

opened	prepared	rained
closed	loved	stayed
cleaned	showed	called
played	smiled	entered

It rained last Sunday and she stayed home.

She opened the door and he entered.

He showed her the photograph and she smiled.

t

asked	crossed	washed	talked
danced	walked	liked	chased
laughed	worked	looked	watched

Linda laughed and danced all night.

They watched television and talked about football.

Jack walked to the library and looked at magazines.

CHAPTER SEVEN

e

hotel	left	president
weekend	pet	September
forget	attend	seldom
chess	when	expression

The president went to Mexico in September.

Fred seldom gets dressed before seven.

ey

grade	radiator	favorite
shape	education	dangerous
late	conversation	game
table	mistake	sale

Take the vase from the table.

Jane made a cake for David.

VOCABULARY

CHAPTER ONE

alone	early	magician	Saturday	way
always	easy	most	seldom	weather
	education	motorcycle	shave (v.)	word
banana	ever		sing	worried
because		never	sometimes	
before	feed		speak	
bench		often	sports car	
bored	half		subject	
	hypnotist	pigeon		
college		politics	tired	
conversation	know			
		quiet	understand	
downtown	late		usually	
during	live (v.)	record		
	lonely	responsibility		

Expressions

early	in a hurry	free time
late	a part-time job	a good time
on time	all kinds of things	most of the time

CHAPTER TWO

air	employee	information	radiator	tennis
amusing	experience			tie (n.)
		jeans	shorts	tire (n.)
because	fantastic	just	something	town
	foreign		stop	
center		lose	storekeeper	unusual
closet	gas	lucky	sugar	useful
company	glove		suit	
conversation	grade (n.)	main course	swimsuit	
customer				win (v.)
	high	nightclub	tea	would
driver	high heels		tell	
		order (v.)		
		other		

Expressions

Make yourself at home.
Take good care of your car.

He meets people on the job.
The garage is in the center
of town.

There aren't any left.
That's too bad!

Is that all?
You're just lucky.

CHAPTER THREE

afterwards	dangerous	golf	pair	toothpaste
already	dessert		parent	towel
appetite	drum	hold (v.)	poetry	trumpet
	dry			type (v.)
boss		language	regular	
bus fare	empty			use (v.)
	except	metro	safe	
can (v.)	expect		same	Wednesday
checkers		nearby	sauce	weight
chess	fast	need (v.)	shampoo	wet
clothes	feed		slow	
comfortable	fix	oil	song	
crowded	flute	onion	swim	
		order (n.)		
			tank	

Expressions

What's the matter?
That's nice of you.

I hope not.
I don't think so.

I'm afraid so.

CHAPTER FOUR

boring	fisherman	leather	rain (v.)	traveler's checks
borrow (v.)	fly (v.)	luck	raincoat	
bucket			receptionist	without
	glasses	map		wood
catch		marvelous	sell	
catfish	haircut	medium	sick	zoo
	happiness		size	
everywhere		perfume	smart	
exercise (v.)	jacket	pond	smell (v.)	
			start (v.)	

Expressions

I'm sorry.
I'm glad.

Of course.
No problem.

No fishing.
Sure, mister.

Lots of
Mmm . . .

CHAPTER FIVE

anyone	hate (v.)	narrow	successful	warm
awful	housework	noisy	sunny	weather
				weekend
chore	iron (v.)	pastry	temperature	windy
cloudy		play (n.)	terrible	workaholic
	last (adj.)	provide	toy	
damp			transportation	yesterday
degree	market	rain (n.)	travel (v.)	
discuss	model	report	trip	
	mop (v.)	represent	truth	
factory	most	representative		
farm (n.)		return	vacuum (v.)	
fly (v.)				

Expressions

They went by car.   Welcome back.   All over Europe.
He was sick in bed.   Take out the trash.

CHAPTER SIX

African	delicious	find	peaceful	visit (n.)
after	disagree	flamenco	peas	visit (v.)
agree		fresh air	play (n.)	volleyball
	end (v.)			
basket	enter	later	see	
boring				
	film	miss (v.)	uncomfortable	
carry	finally	musician	unfortunately	
chess				

Expressions

Are you new in town?   all day   Boy . . .
Welcome to Sunnyville.   all night   Say . . .
It's right down the street.   old times

CHAPTER SEVEN

accurately	careful	happily	photographer	slowly
actress	carefully		premier	soft
announcer	carnation	invite		speaker
anxiously	clearly		quick	star
attend	crowd	loud	quickly	suitcase
autograph				
	excite	mistake	reader	then
back			relax	tomorrow
badly	florist	pack (v.)		typist
	flour	perfectly	show (n.)	
	follow	perhaps	sign (v.)	worker
				writer

Expressions

Why not?

CHAPTER EIGHT

admire	clever	hard hat	nobody	send
answering	cologne	hope (v.)		shopping bag
machine	continue		ocean	shy
anything	cosmetics	journey		
appear	couple		pastime	teahouse
appointment		land (v.)	perfect	teapot
	disappear	learn	plane	than
better	disgusting	leather	pull (v.)	thousand
boat		lipstick		together
boring	everyone	long distance	quite	turn off
borrow	eye shadow	lovely		
bother (v.)			rubber glove	voice
broken	frog legs	message		
	funny	mile	sail (v.)	world
	furniture	mountain	samba	
		mysterious	selfish	

Expressions

What's wrong?	He doesn't look very well.	Watch out!
What's your problem?	It's really bothering him.	How do you get around?
See you tomorrow.	That's fine.	Well . . .
I'm going to cash a check.	That's true.	Me too.

Physical Problems

backache	sore throat	cold
earache	stomachache	
headache	toothache	